The Book of Esther

*The Visible Acts of the Invisible God – A
Study in the Providence of God*

Charlie Avila

The material in this book was first taught in a Fresno School of Ministry class offered at our church and presented on the teacherofthebible.com website in the United States.

Clovis Christian Center
3606 N. Fowler Ave
Fresno, California, USA 93727-1124

Copyright © 2019 Charlie Avila

ISBN: **9781795537476**

Printed in the United States

CONTENTS

DEDICATION

This book is affectionately dedicated to Pastor Ron and Paula Hemphill. They are dedicated servants of the Lord, faithful and loyal to God and His people, and gifted spiritual leaders over their flock in Oregon. They inspired me to study Esther and this book is the result of their encouragement. Thank you.

PREFACE

Recently, a storm swept through our city. There was no rain, thunder, lightning, or hail. It was only wind. You could hear the wind whistling through the trees. The trees were bent over. Branches broke off. Dust was swirling everywhere. Objects were flying through the air. The next day, we saw the damage on the streets. Trees were overturned; branches and trash were on all the roads; debris could be seen at every turn – all because of a strong wind!

Jesus told Nicodemus in John 3:8, "The wind blows wherever it pleases. You hear its sound, but you cannot tell where it comes from or where it is going." Wind cannot be seen, but its impact is surely felt. The wind is invisible.

In the Book of Esther, God is like a mighty wind. He is never mentioned by name in any verse. The words, "God," "Lord," or "Jehovah" are never seen, but His impact is felt in every chapter. God is invisible, but His actions are not – they are clearly seen. The main character in the Book of Esther is not Mordecai, Haman, Esther or the king. Dr. Terry Muck wrote, "Read correctly, the lead character of the book of Esther is not even Esther, but God."

Pastor Ray Stedman reminds us, "As you read through the book of Esther, you will see that God is not absent. Invisible, yes; absent, no. His actions are on every page and in every line. Just beneath the surface of the story is another story. It's the story of how God works behind the scenes of our lives to accomplish His purposes." Chuck Swindoll says, "He's absolutely invisible. Yet He is at work!"

In Chapter 1, the Lord removed Vashti as queen. In Chapter 2, the Lord made sure that a Jewish orphan was selected as queen of the greatest empire at that time. God's favor allowed Esther to be picked from among thousands of beautiful women. God made sure that the king forgot to honor Mordecai for thwarting an assassination plot for a more opportune time. In Chapter 3, God made sure that the "lot" landed on a certain day to give the Jews eleven months to prepare their defense.

In Chapter 4, God gave Esther and Mordecai a go-between so that her Jewish identity could be kept secret. In Chapter 5, the Lord gave Esther favor before the king even though he had not seen her in thirty days. God arranged for Haman to build a gallows to hang Mordecai on the day before the king was to honor him. In Chapter 6, God made sure that the king had a sleepless night, and when his servants went to get some reading material, these servants picked Mordecai's heroic deed from among thousands of records. The Lord insured that there was perfect timing between Haman wanting Mordecai dead and the king wanting Mordecai honored.

In Chapter 7, God placed Harbonah right next to the king so he could tell the king where to hang Haman. In Chapter 8, the Lord gave both Esther and Mordecai favor before the king so he could tell them to write a decree that would counter Haman's decree. In Chapter 9, the very day that Haman picked for the annihilation of the Jews turned into a Jewish celebration called "Purim." What was meant for evil, God turned around for good. In Chapter 10, God took a Jewish exile and placed him as second in command over the Persian Empire. God is good!

Commentator Mervin Breneman is surely correct: "There is only one conclusion that can be reached when the book is read: God was behind it all."

The Book of Esther has been a favorite of Jews and Christians for centuries. May the Lord give you insight, revelation, and wisdom as you study this powerful book. Like Moses when he forsook Egypt, may you "see Him who is invisible" (Hebrews 11:27). May you see the glory of God in Esther.

Jesus Christ is Lord. To God be the glory.
Charlie Avila, September 2019

Esther: An Introduction

"I make known the end from the beginning, from ancient times, what is still to come. I say: My purpose will stand, and I will do all that I please." (Isaiah 46:10)

The book of Esther is one of the few books in the Bible that does not mention God, Lord, or Jehovah by name in any verse. Simply put, God is not mentioned. And yet, you can see His powerful action behind the scenes. In verse after verse of Esther, you see *the visible acts of the invisible God.* As Pastor Ray Stedman writes, "As you read through the book of Esther, you will see that God is not absent. Invisible, yes; absent, no. His actions are on every page and in every line."[1] One commentator notes, "That God or Lord does not appear in the Book of Esther is not an accident. It is intentional. This is the way the Holy Spirit wanted the book. The Lord wanted all of us to see that even though He is not named, He is there

---

[1] *For Such a Time as This:* Secrets of Strategic Living from the Book of Esther, Ray C. Stedman, Discovery House Publishers, Grand Rapids, Michigan, page 14.

working in the lives of His people. The complete absence of God from the text is the genius of the book."[2]

Perhaps the greatest truth in the Book of Esther is what Christians call the providence of God. What does that mean?

The providence of God means the wisdom, care, and guidance provided by God. That He is "the caring force" guiding all the affairs of mankind. In other words, the Lord is reigning sovereignly over all the activities, dealings, and events in human life and history, and He is bringing them to His desired end and purpose. The will of God is going to prevail over all demons, humans, and natural forces. In the end, God always wins.

In order for this to be true, and it is, God must know the end from the beginning. He has to be omniscient, omnipotent, and omnipresent; that is all-knowing, all-powerful, and all-present. God knows everything about everything. He is the Lord God Almighty. The prophet said, "I make known the end from the beginning, from ancient times, what is still to come. I say: My purpose will stand, and I will do all that I please."[3]

The definition of providence is very insightful. "Pro" is a prefix that means "in advance; before; in front; from the beginning" and "videre" or "videntia" means "sight" or "vision." It means "foresight" or "to see in advance."

It's the same definition as "to provide" or "provision." You see things in advance, and you make provision for it. Joseph, by the revelation of God's Spirit, saw the famine coming in advance and he made provision (Genesis 41). God is Jehovah-Jireh, my Provider, so He had a ram waiting for Abraham even before he went to the top of

---

[2] *Esther*, Karen H. Jobes, The NIV Application Commentary, Zondervan Publishers, Grand Rapids, Michigan, page 42.
[3] See Isaiah 46:10, New International Version (NIV).

the mountain to sacrifice his son, Isaac (Genesis 22). The Lord had a large fish waiting for Jonah even though he was disobedient and running from God (Jonah 1).

One final word related to providence is "foreknowledge." This means "to know in advance or before it happens." Notice how it is used in the New Testament: Acts 2:22-23 – "Jesus of Nazareth...delivered up by the determined purpose and *foreknowledge* of God..." 1 Peter 1:1-2 – "To God's elect...who have been chosen according to the *foreknowledge* of God the Father..."

The Greek word here for "foreknowledge" in both verses is "prognōsis." "Pro" means "before; beginning; in front" and "gnōsis" is the main Greek word for "knowledge." The bottom-line – God knows in advance what is going to happen. He already knows before it happens. Moreover, He is moving people, things, events, and circumstances into place in advance to fulfill His purposes.

When the doctor gives you a "prognosis," it means that he already knows in advance how things are probably going to work out. They have seen so many cases of the same thing that they can pretty much tell you what's going to happen in your case. Although doctors are limited in their knowledge and they are speaking out of experience, God is unlimited in His knowledge and He is speaking prophetically to accomplish His purpose and His will.

A Personal Story of God's Providence

God knows everything in advance. He moves people into places and positions whether they know it or not. My wife and I got married by the supernatural providence of God. To bring us together, the Lord did many miracles well in advance of our meeting in person. No one could do this but God.

I'll let my wife tell the story.

I (Irma) came to the United States from Mexico in July of 1963. I did not come over under good circumstances. My father, who was a terrible womanizer, was caught whistling at a girl as she walked down the street with her boyfriend. The boyfriend became enraged and attacked my dad with a long knife. The man wounded him so badly that he actually died on the operating table at a local hospital. Miraculously, he was revived, and eventually survived the brutal attack.

A young married couple, friends of my dad, Reynaldo and Rosie, called my mom in Mexico and told her about my dad's situation. My mom then brought my older sister and me across the border to see my dad. Because we had nowhere to stay, we moved into Rosie's house. I should say right now, that this same Rosie, nearly twenty years later, would lead Charlie's dad and mom to the Lord.

Thank God, my dad survived. My parents ended up having four more children – a total of five girls and one boy. As it turned out, I was the only one in my family who became a Christian. I was twenty years old when I first surrendered my life to Jesus Christ as my personal Lord and Savior.

My older sister got married at the young age of twenty. I was her maiden of honor. My best friend, Maria, got married at twenty-three. I was also the maiden of honor at her wedding. Furthermore, I attended many weddings of family and friends, and I was in the wedding parties for several couples. To top it off, my younger sister, who was twelve years younger than I was, already had a boyfriend who would later become her husband. I was hurt and had jealous feelings, but not because of him, but because of me – why was I being passed up? My other sisters, who were also younger, had boyfriends.

So here I am, the only Christian believer, and everyone but me is getting married and finding boyfriends. Even non-Christian family and friends were getting married before me. Honestly, because I was getting older, I was becoming anxious and worried. Would I ever marry? Would I ever have children? I even entertained the thought of adopting a child – as a single woman – so I could be a mother.

Another situation arose that made me uncomfortable. There was a man in my church that appeared to be available. Several of the ladies in our church told me that he might be a potential match for me. When I found out that he had been married twice before and had adult children, I knew I didn't want a relationship with him. Maria, my best friend, also told me that he was definitely not the right man for me. I was thankful for her confirmation.

I started thinking to myself, "You need to pray harder. You need to make this a priority and ask God earnestly in prayer." With an anxious and burdened heart, I got on my knees and cried out in a loud voice for God's direction and leading. I remember one time praying so loud that my mom heard me and became so concerned for me that she came running into my room and asked if I was okay.

At this time, I was talking very openly and honestly with the Lord. "What is Your will for my life? Do You want me to remain single? If You want me to stay single all my life, then take away any desire for a husband." Somehow, I trusted the Lord to take away any feelings that were not from Him. I continued to pray regularly about my future and about my husband.

I reached a very important juncture in this whole process. I felt like I needed support from other Christians. But whom could I talk to about something so personal? I developed confidence to go speak with Rosie. She had been like a spiritual mom to me, and she knew my family and my life probably better than anyone. She was a woman, had been a Christian for many years, and I trusted her judgment. Rosie could help me bear this burden.

I called Rosie and went to her house. I shared my apprehensions and concerns with her. I was actually quite embarrassed to tell her how I was feeling, but somehow it all came out. She listened patiently as I talked and cried. Many tears went down my cheeks as I unburdened my soul before her.

I'll never forget what happened next. She got up from where she was sitting, went to a room and came back with a brand-new, bathroom hand towel (pictured). She also  brought a black, Sharpie permanent marker. Rosie read the prayer of Psalm 86. She then told me to write down "Psalm 86" on the towel and today's date – 5-6-1989 (for May 6, 1989). We prayed in agreement that if God wanted me to have a husband that he would come forth – even out of the closet if need be! One of the reasons that Rosie brought the towel was to wipe away all the tears that I was crying. I left her house very tired.

EVEN THOUGH I HAD NEVER MET CHARLIE OR EVEN KNEW THAT SUCH A PERSON EXISTED, I FOUND OUT LATER THAT MAY 6TH WAS CHARLIE'S BIRTHDAY! When I learned this fact, it really assured my heart.

Exactly three weeks later, Rosie wanted to go to Charlie's house because one of his brothers was graduating from the university and several of his brothers were in town to attend his graduation ceremony. Originally, Rosie's son was going to give her a ride to Charlie's house, but at the last minute, his work called him in, and she ended up calling me to give her a ride. I believe this was a divine rearrangement. God was working out the details so I could meet my future husband. So I took Rosie to Charlie's house. It was May 27th, exactly three weeks after I prayed at Rosie's house. I would later realize that Rosie, the person who housed my mom, my sister, and me back in the early 1960s, was the same person who led Charlie's family to the Lord in the early 1980s. God was at work decades in advance! He is the supernatural matchmaker.

To make a long story short, I met my husband at the house of a lady whom Rosie had led to the Lord. In less than two years, Charlie and I would be married. Although God was not seen physically, His supernatural acts were clearly evident. I thank God for what He did in my life! God's providence is real!

I thank God for my wife's heart-felt testimony. The Lord sent Irma to the United States and she stayed with Rosie back in the 1960's, and this same lady would lead my parents to the Lord in the 1980's. We met in 1989. We got married in 1991. The Lord was arranging everything – decades in advance – so that we could be together. This is God's providence at work. Irma and I are together today because of the visible acts of the invisible God.

This is what excites me as we approach the Book of Esther. Along with the Song of Solomon, this is the only book in the Bible that doesn't mention God or Lord by name. It also doesn't say anything about prayer, the temple, Jerusalem, Jewish sacrifices, nor any apocalyptic vision like we find in Daniel.

However, in every chapter, you see the invisible hand of God. In every chapter, you see God at work. In every chapter, you see that God is not absent, but present. In every chapter, you see not coincidence, but providence. Upon further examination, we see the Lord working out His purpose, accomplishing His plan, keeping His promises, doing everything according to the counsel of His will, and surely, He foresaw everything in the Book of Esther. In advance, beforehand, at the beginning, He maneuvered everything into place, often years in advance, to fulfill what He wanted and what He pleased. God is sovereign. God reigns in the heavens.

So as Christians, we don't believe in coincidence, but providence. As Christian believers we don't believe in nor do we trust in luck or random happenings or things happening by chance or blind fate. Chuck Swindoll says, "Take the word 'coincidental' out of your vocabulary, along with 'luck.' You can trash them both! You don't need them anymore. Nothing is coincidental! 'Luck' has no place in a Christian's vocabulary."[4]

So the theme of this book is *The Visible Acts of the Invisible God.* "We are right to ask, 'If all of these allusions and coincidences point to the God of biblical history, why is he NOT named?' Perhaps it is not so much the PRESENCE of God but the HIDDENNESS of God in human events that the story articulates. To be hidden is to be present yet unseen. What is visible is only the human side of the story. Perceiving something beyond or behind takes faith."[5]

The Persian Empire & Its Kings

The events in the Book of Esther took place nearly 2,500 years ago (483-473 B.C.) in a foreign land (Persia) under a world-dominating kingdom. This empire was founded by Cyrus the Great around 550 B.C. and ended in 331 B.C. after they were defeated by Alexander the Great and the Greeks.

The Book of Daniel again allows us to see God's incredible "provision" and "prognosis" – He sees in advance and He knows in advance. God gave Nebuchadnezzar a dream to see hundreds of years into the future. This is the foreknowledge of God.

The Persian Empire in Daniel 2: The 2nd part of the image was "chest and arms of silver" (Daniel 2:32). It was a kingdom that would be "inferior" to the Babylonian kingdom (Daniel 2:39).

---

[4] *Esther: A Woman of Strength & Dignity*, Charles R. Swindoll, Word Publishing, Nashville, Tennessee, page 127.
[5] *Ezra, Nehemiah, Esther*, Leslie Allen and Timothy Laniak, New International Biblical Commentary, Hendrickson Publishers, Peabody, Massachusetts, page 185.

The Persian Empire in Daniel 7: Daniel had "a dream and visions" (Daniel 7:1) where he saw the four winds stir up the Great Sea and four beasts rose up. These four beasts match the four parts of the statue of Nebuchadnezzar's dream. The 2nd beast was a bear that was raised up on one side and had three ribs in its mouth. It was told to "Arise, devour much flesh" (Daniel 7:5).

The Persian Empire in Daniel 8: Daniel had another vision in which he saw himself "in Shushan, the citadel, which is in the province of Elam" (Daniel 8:2). The prophet saw a ram with two horns, one was "higher than the other," and the higher one came up last. Gabriel tells Daniel specifically that "the ram which you saw, having the two horns – they are the kings of Media and Persia" (Daniel 8:20).

These dreams and visions and their interpretations reveal that God knew the Medo-Persian Empire would arise after the Babylonian kingdom. God saw everything in advance. In fact, He was the One who would raise up these kings and their kingdom. He saw the chest and arms of silver; the bear with the ribs in its mouth; and the ram with two horns. The Lord described the very nature of this kingdom even before it existed. 2 Chronicles 36:20 says, "And those who escaped from the sword Nebuchadnezzar carried away to Babylon, where they became servants to him and his sons *until the rule of the kingdom of Persia*."

For this study on Esther, let's look quickly at three Persian kings that ruled one right after another.

Darius (522-486 B.C.) – This king was the father of the king in Esther. He is featured prominently in the books of Ezra, Haggai and Zechariah.

- Ezra 4:5 – "…the *reign of Darius* king of Persia."
- Haggai 1:1 – "In the second year of *King Darius*…"

- Zechariah 1:1 – "In the eighth month of the second year of *Darius*, the word of the Lord came to Zechariah…"

Ahasuerus (485-464 B.C.) – This is the king of Esther. He is known more by his Greek name, "Xerxes." He was the son of Darius. Other than the 29 times that he appears by name in the Book of Esther, he is only mentioned once in Ezra:

- Ezra 4:6 – "In the reign of *Ahasuerus*, in the beginning of his reign, they wrote an accusation against the inhabitants of Judah and Jerusalem."

Artaxerxes (464-424 B.C.) – He was the son of Ahasuerus and grandson of Darius. He is in the book of Ezra, and Nehemiah was the cupbearer of this king.

- Ezra 7:12-13 – "*Artaxerxes, king of kings*, to Ezra the priest, a scribe of the Law of the God of heaven: Perfect peace, and so forth. I issue a decree that all those of the people of Israel and the priests and Levites in my realm, who volunteer to go up to Jerusalem, may go with you."
- Nehemiah 2:1 – "And it came to pass in the month of Nisan, in the twentieth year of *King Artaxerxes*, when wine was before him, that I took the wine and gave it to the king."

Main Themes of the Book of Esther

Part of the problem for the average Christian in studying the Book of Esther are the strange names and their functions and the dates and their meanings. Often, we read names and terms that are not familiar to us:

- Esther 1:10 – "...Mehuman, Biztha, Harbona, Bigtha, Abagtha, Zethar, and Carcas, seven eunuchs..."
- Esther 1:14 – "...Carshena, Shethar, Admatha, Tarshish, Meres, Marsena, and Memucan, the seven princes..."
- Esther 9:7-9 – "Parshandatha, Dalphon, Aspatha, Poratha, Adalia, Aridatha, Parmashta, Arisai, Aridai, and Vajezatha..." (the ten sons of Haman)

Haman's father was "Hammedatha" and his wife was "Zeresh." There were various servants like "Hegai," "Shaashgaz," "Hathach," and "Harbonah." The king's name was "Ahasuerus" and Esther's Hebrew name was "Hadassah." The two men who tried to assassinate the king are "Bigthan" and "Teresh."

Another problem are the months. When exactly are "Tebeth," "Nisan," "Sivan," and "Adar?" English readers are not familiar with these words.

The words "day(s)," "month(s)," and "year(s)" are mentioned seventy-five times in Esther. Dates will become very important for certain decrees and the Feast of Purim in Chapter 9.

- Esther 9:18 – "...on the thirteenth day, as well as on the fourteenth; and on the fifteenth of the month..."
- Esther 9:21 – "...they should celebrate yearly the fourteenth and fifteenth days of the month of Adar..."

There are three critical times in the first three chapters of Esther. We will study these dates carefully in the commentary:

- Esther 1:3 – "...in the *third year of his reign*..." (3rd Year)

- Esther 2:16 – "…in the tenth month, which is the month of Tebeth, in the *seventh year of his reign…*" (7th Year)
- Esther 3:7 – "In the first month, which is the month of Nisan, in the *twelfth year of King Ahasuerus…*" (12th Year)

From Chapters 1 through 3, nine to ten years transpire. Prior to studying the Book of Esther for this book and a class that I taught, no one had ever explained to me that the first three chapters cover a time span of nearly ten years. Knowing these years really opens up our understanding of Esther.

One of the prominent features of Esther are the feasts. There are three feasts in Chapter 1: The 180-day feast (1:4), the 7-day feast (1:5), and Queen Vashti's feast (1:9). There are three feasts for or by Queen Esther: "The king made a great feast, the Feast of Esther…" (2:18), the first "banquet of wine" (5:6), and the second "banquet of wine" (7:2, 7:7, and 7:8). The Feast of Purim: This will become the yearly feast that is celebrated even today by Jews around the world, usually in the month of March for two days. "They made it a day of feasting and gladness" (9:18), "gladness and feasting, as a holiday" (9:19), and "they should make them days of feasting and joy" (9:22). Because there is so much feasting, the fasting will stand out even more (4:3, 4:16, 9:31).

"Decrees" play key roles in the book of Esther. The Persians loved decrees. Cyrus issued a decree for the Jews to return to build the house of God (Ezra 5:13). Darius issued a decree to verify that Cyrus issued a decree (Ezra 6:1)! Darius issued another decree for people to help the Jews who were returning (Ezra 6:8). Darius issued a decree that if anyone altered the decree he should be hanged (Ezra 6:11)! Artaxerxes issued a decree that anyone who wanted to return to Jerusalem with Ezra the priest and scribe could do so (Ezra 7:12-13). Artaxerxes issued another decree for people to support and supply Ezra and his travelers with what they needed for the trip home. (Ezra 7:21). Don't forget that 30-day decree issued by Darius the Mede in Daniel 6 that eventually landed the prophet in the lions' den.

In the Book of Esther, there are at least six decrees: The decree that banishes Vashti and that all women should respect their husbands (1:19-22). The Miss Persia Beauty Pageant decree (2:8). Haman's decree to destroy the Jews (3:9, 3:12, 3:15, 4:3, 4:8, 9:1). Mordecai's decree for the Jews to defend themselves against Haman's decree (8:8-17). The king's decree for the Jews to defend themselves on the fourteenth day of Adar (the day after) and for Haman's ten sons to be hanged (9:13-15). The "decree of Esther" to confirm the continual feasts of Purim (9:31-32).

With these simple summary statements about the Book of Esther, let's go to Chapter 1, where God is already at work, removing one queen to make way for another.

THE BOOK OF ESTHER

1

Queen Vashi & The Persian Empire

"Vashti shall come no more before King
Ahasuerus; and let the king give her royal
position to another who is better than she."
(Esther 1:19)

It is amazing that God knew in advance that
Haman would issue a horrific decree to annihilate
all the Jews in the "twelfth year of King
Ahasuerus" (3:7), so nine years earlier, the Lord removes the
present queen, Vashti, and makes preparations for Esther to
ascend the throne as queen. Vashti is removed "in the third
year of his reign" (1:3). The Lord is already moving people
into place well before they are needed.

The first chapter of Esther lays the foundation for all
the people, places and events of the rest of the book. We see
a vast empire, a wealthy king, royal feasts, decrees, princes
and eunuchs, and even the king's anger. The first chapter
sets the stage for all the other chapters.

Esther 1:1 reads, "Now it came to pass in the days of Ahasuerus (this was the Ahasuerus who reigned over one hundred and twenty-seven provinces, from India to Ethiopia)." Ahasuerus is more commonly known by his Greek name, Xerxes, and most modern translations use that word. I will use "Ahasuerus" throughout this commentary simply because the Persian name, "Achashverowsh," is what is used in the Hebrew text.

Both this verse and Esther 8:9 identify the vastness of Ahasuerus' reign – it had 127 provinces. When Mordecai issued his decree in Chapter 8, it went out to "...the princes of the provinces from India to Ethiopia, one hundred and twenty-seven provinces in all..." "India"[6] is where modern day Pakistan is located. This was the farthest eastern section of the Persian Empire. "Ethiopia" is literally "Kuwsh" or "Cush." It is located in modern Sudan. This is the southernmost tip of this empire. Some places of the empire are more than 2,000 miles from Shushan the capital. These distances will be important as we look at the empire-wide decrees that happen in the Book of Esther.

Remember that right after the Babylonian Empire fell, "Darius the Mede" took over and he "set one hundred and twenty satraps"[7] over his kingdom. This was about 60-70 years before Esther 1:1. Each satrap was over one province. So it is accurate that the Medo-Persian Empire could have expanded or been broken up by seven additional provinces in that amount of time.

Verse 2 simply tells us where the headquarters or "the throne" was located in the vast empire. It was located in "Shushan" or "Susa." It was a "citadel," or "biyrah," which is a Persian word that means "palace" or "castle." "Shushan" appears nineteen times in Esther, and it will be

---

[6] Literally in Hebrew, "Hodu," or "Hindu-stan." It appears only here and in Esther 8:9 in the entire Bible.
[7] See Daniel 6:1.

the key place for all the decrees and main battles in this great story. We'll say more about "Shushan" as it appears in the commentary.

According to Laniak, "Xerxes had four capitals. Susa was his primary one, and its citadel served as his winter/spring palace."[8] When Daniel saw the vision of the ram with two horns (the Medo-Persian Empire), he "was in Shushan, the citadel, which is in the province of Elam."[9] This is also where Nehemiah was living when he was the cupbearer to King Artaxerxes: "I was in Shushan the citadel."[10]

One of the most important words in this first chapter is the Hebrew word, "malkut" or literally "of his kingdom" (v2). As one commentator explains, "A key term throughout this scene is 'malkut,' an adjective translated 'royal' six times (1:2, 7, 9, 11, 19 (twice)) and a noun translated 'kingdom/realm' three times (1:4, 14, 20)."[11] Everything of royalty was tied to this kingdom: "Royal wine" (v7), "royal palace" (v9), "royal crown" (v11), "royal decree" and "royal position" (v19). The "kingdom" and "empire" are synonymous terms that describe the "reign of King Ahasuerus."

Verse 3 describes the first of three "feasts" in Chapter 1. This feast was for the "nobles," "princes," or "the powers of Persia and Media." They were the king's officials and servants. This feast took place in "the third year of his reign" or 483 B.C.

It is important to ask why did this king have a feast that lasted "one hundred and eighty days in all." They had a massive party that lasted about six months! What was the purpose of such an extravagant feast? He was trying to show these government officials and military commanders "the

---

[8] See Laniak, page 194.
[9] See Daniel 8:2.
[10] See Nehemiah 1:1.
[11] See Laniak, page 198.

riches of his glorious kingdom and the splendor of his excellent majesty" (v4). Why?

Darius (522-486 B.C.) was the father of Ahasuerus. He was the king who features prominently in Ezra, Haggai, and Zechariah. There were many battles between the Persians and the Greeks in his years. In 490 B.C., there was the famous battle at Marathon where the Greeks decisively defeated the Persians, even though the Persians had superior numbers in both army and navy. Legend says that a man named Pheidippides, who was a Greek herald in that battle, ran from Marathon to Athens to announce the glorious victory over the Persians. He ran for a little over 26 miles, which defines the distance of our modern track and field marathons.

Anyway, this humiliating defeat in 490 B.C. demoralized the Persians. Darius died in 486 B.C. and his son took over. This feast took place three years later, "in the third year of his reign," to drum up support from all of his government and military leaders, along with another "feast for all the people present in Shushan" (v5). He needed the support of his people for another major battle that was going to take place in 480 B.C. (Another battle, by the way, where the Persians would be defeated by the Greeks.) King Ahasuerus pulled all the stops. He wanted the most extravagant and lavish feasts the empire had ever seen. Even though his father and military were soundly defeated, it would not happen again under his watch.

This, incidentally, is why Vashti's disobedience was such a disaster for King Ahasuerus. In the eyes of the king and his people, Vashti's rejection of the king rained fire and brimstone on the king's parade and feasts. Just when the king was seeking the support of all his subjects, the very queen in his palace is rejecting him publicly. This irreverent act was a humiliating slap on the king's face. The action against her was swift and decisive. Vashti's reign as queen came to a sudden and disastrous end.

When this feast of 180 days was over, "the king made a feast lasting seven days for all the people who were present in Shushan the citadel, from great to small, in the court of the garden of the king's palace." This feast for the commoners and soldiers in the capital was intended to keep everyone and everything positive. He needed everyone's support for the coming battle. Let's keep everybody happy with lots of food, wine, and song. He needs everybody behind him for the military campaign of 480 B.C. Let's get everyone behind the king and what he is doing.

This feast was held for only seven days "in the court of the garden," which is probably the same place known as the "palace garden" where the king goes to try to cool off in his rage against Haman (7:7-8).

Verse 6 tries to describe the beauty and luxury of the palace surroundings. "There were white and blue linen curtains fastened with cords of fine linen and purple on silver rods and marble pillars; and the couches were of gold and silver on a mosaic pavement of alabaster, turquoise, and white and black marble." Wow! Gold and silver. Marble and turquoise. Beautiful colors. Only the finest linens, pillars, and pavement will do. He was showing off the "splendor" of his "glorious kingdom" and "excellent majesty." No expense was spared.

Moreover, the drinking glasses ("vessels") were made of gold and no two were the same. There was nothing generic or cookie-cutter here. Everything was one of a kind. Everything was expensive. These were handcrafted items that only a wealthy king could afford. As Baldwin notes, "These Persian goblets of gold were individually designed and beautifully decorated."[12] These goblets were filled with "royal wine in abundance" (v7). He let everyone drink whatever they wanted. This was no cheap wine; this was

---

[12] *Esther*, Joyce G. Baldwin, Tyndale Old Testament Commentaries, Inter-Varsity Press, Downers Grove, Illinois, page 58.

"royal wine." Only the best wine from the finest vineyards was used. I'm sure many people got drunk on this "royal wine," for even the king himself "was merry with wine" (v10). All of this extravagance was part of the "generosity of the king." The king is holding nothing back from his people. He is making sure that everyone is happy and satisfied.

Since the Persian Empire was governed by laws and decrees, they had to have a law for drinking. This law said that you could drink as much or as little as each person determined. One translation of Esther 1:8 reads, "By edict of the king, no limits were placed on the drinking, for the king had instructed all his palace officials to serve each man as much as he wanted." "His guests could drink a lot or a little. And if they didn't want to drink at all, that was fine, too. Each individual could do as he wished in the midst of the banqueting and revelry."[13] Basically, here was a law that said you could be lawless! The king was giving everyone complete liberty and freedom to do whatever they wanted. Don't put any restraints or limits on anyone. Let people do whatever pleases them. This is what will keep everyone happy with the king and his kingdom. Again, the king wants everyone on his side for the upcoming military campaigns.

The men were having a great time in the palace and its exquisite surroundings. What about the women? Well, they had a "feast" too.

Verse 9 says, "Queen Vashti also made a feast for the women in the royal palace which belonged to King Ahasuerus." This is now the third feast of Chapter 1, and the first mention of Vashti in the Bible. One commentator says that "Vashti" means "the beloved" or "the desired one."[14] There is no doubt that Vashti was "beautiful to behold"

---

[13] See Swindoll, page 25.
[14] See Baldwin, page 60.

(1:11). She was a gorgeous woman with a beautiful face and body.

Obviously, back in that Persian culture, there was the separation of the sexes. Even today, in the Indian and Persian cultures, men and women sit on opposite sides of a building or church. Somehow, the writer of Esther wants everyone to know that although Vashti has her own "feast for the women," that feast is being held in "the royal palace that belongs to King Ahasuerus." The queen is using what belongs to the king. She is not independent of him.

Before we move into verse 10 and following, I want to say something about eunuchs, concubines, harems, and the culture of that time.

There are many instances where believers of the 21st Century try to impose Christian morals back on an ancient text and a foreign culture. The word, "eunuch(s)," is found twelve times in Esther and three times in this first chapter (1:10, 12, 15). It is a Greek word that means "eunē" (bed) + "echein" (to keep; to hold). "Eunuch" literally means a castrated man who guards or keeps the king's bed. Herodotus, the Greek historian, tells us that the Persian kings had up to 360 concubines at their disposal, one for every day of the year. A beautiful woman could be summoned to his palace each night for his sexual pleasure. Under penalty of death, no king was ever denied by one of his concubines. As horrible as this appears from a Christian and a moral standpoint, this was the reality of the Book of Esther. The king's harem lived in a dormitory, and they were there to meet any desires he had. This was not God's standard nor a biblical standard, but a Persian standard. From a Christian view, Vashti's refusal to appear before the king and his audience may be viewed as a heroic act of morality and holiness, but to the people of her day, it was an act of deep personal betrayal and rejection.

Verse 10 starts with "on the seventh day…" The "feast that lasted seven days" of verse 5 had now come to an end. The king was probably a little drunk. He was feeling good. "The heart of the king was merry with wine." This is the last day of all the feasting – "the seventh day." He has pulled out all the stops. He's put forth the best of everything and "in abundance" (1:7).

What can be the final, ultimate display of his glory and majesty? What is most impressive? It is his beautiful queen. In verse 4, he wanted "*to show* the riches of his glorious kingdom"; and now, in verse 11, he wants "*to show* her beauty to the people and the officials." The king has one last opportunity to "show off." The "greatest show on earth" must end with a stunning display of the queen's beauty.

He "commanded" seven eunuchs "who served in the presence of King Ahasuerus" to bring Queen Vashti. I don't want to lose sight of that key word, "commanded." The king is exercising his authority as supreme ruler over the Persian Empire. This is a commandment. There are no other options. She must come. Anything less is an act of rebellion in his eyes. Notice the strong wording found in the remaining text – "Queen Vashti refused to come at the king's *command*" (v12), "she did not obey the *command* of King Ahasuerus" (v15), and "King Ahasuerus *commanded* Queen Vashti to be brought in before him" (v17). Vashti disobeyed a direct command of the king. Her fate was sealed.

We all know what happened next. Verse 12 says, "But Queen Vashti refused to come at the king's command brought by his eunuchs; therefore the king was furious, and his anger burned within him." He could control 127 provinces but he could not control the will of one woman. "Vashti ruins with one stroke the effect of the whole ostentatious exhibition."[15] "All of the king's efforts to make a good impression with his lavish banquets are wasted when he decides to exhibit his queen as the epitome of his

---

[15] See T. H. Gaster, page 381.

possessions."[16] This will not be the last time that this king burns in anger. He was "furious." This is unthinkable. This is the ultimate treason. The queen has shamed the king in front of all his people.

First, the king summons "seven eunuchs" to bring Queen Vashti. Now, he summons "seven princes" who are "wise men who understand the times." "The phrase, 'highest in the kingdom,' indicates that this is the best."[17] "Only the seven closest advisors (literally, in Hebrew idiom, 'the seven who see the face of the king') were permitted to enter the king's presence uninvited and unannounced."[18] These men "knew the law and justice" (v13). The king wanted to know what type of action he could take against Vashti that was "according to law" (v15). He now had the experts in front of him to advise him. "What shall we do to Queen Vashti since she did not obey the command of King Ahasuerus?"

One of these "seven princes of Persia and Media" (v15), whom I call "Memucan the Mexican," really expands the gravity and seriousness of the offense. He makes a big problem into a gigantic one. What was a personal grievance between the king and queen, Memucan makes it an empire-wide offense. Notice the language; notice who is offended: "ALL the princes," "ALL the people" in "ALL the provinces" and become "known to ALL the women" and the "ladies" are going to tell "ALL the king's officials" (v18) what Vashti did. Memucan is saying: There is going to be a massive, unrestrained, and diabolic rebellion! We need to stop it right now! He tells the king that "all the women" in the entire Persian Empire "will despise their husbands in their eyes" (v17). There is going to be "excessive contempt

---

[16] See Laniak, page 198.

[17] *Ezra, Nehemiah, Esther*, Mervin Breneman, The New American Commentary, Volume 10, Broadman & Holman Publishers, Nashville, Tennessee, page 309.

[18] See Jobes, page 78. This is unlike Esther's situation in Chapter 5 when she comes into the king's presence uninvited.

and wrath" (v18) in all the Persian homes. Baldwin notes, "The queen defied his majesty, and every husband's authority was threatened."[19] What happens in the palace will begin to take place in the home.

Memucan's recommendation is very simple: "That Vashti shall come no more before King Ahasuerus; and let the king give her royal position to another who is better than she." Vashti's downfall is swift and immediate. She was called "Queen Vashti" (v9), "Queen Vashti" (v11), "Queen Vashti" (v12), "Queen Vashti" (v15), "Queen Vashti" (v16), and "Queen Vashti" (v17). After verse 17, she is only known as "Vashti" (1:19, 2:1, 2:4, and 2:17). She is stripped of her title. Vashti is banished from the king's presence (v19). The party (feast) is over.

In verses 19 and 20, the "royal decree" becomes the "king's decree," and it is the first of many decrees in the Book of Esther. This decree not only decides Vashti's fate, but that "wives will honor their husbands" (v20) and "each man should be master of his own house" (v22).

Let us never lose sight of the main message of Esther – God's providence. Vashti must be removed so the Esther can come forth (2:17). Swindoll describes it as "Exit Vashti; enter Esther."[20] God is at work to get the Jews ready for Haman in Chapter 3 – "Let the king give her royal position to another who is better than she" (v19).

A major part of God's providence and sovereignty is that He raises up kings and He throws them down. The prophet Daniel said, "He removes kings and raises up kings."[21] When Nebuchadnezzar – a very powerful dictator and world ruler – would not acknowledge that God rules over governments, he was told, "...that the living may know that the Most High rules in the kingdom of men, and gives it

---

[19] See Baldwin, page 27.
[20] See Swindoll, page 29.
[21] See Daniel 2:21.

to whomever He will, and sets over it the lowest of men," and again, "...until you know that the Most High rules in the kingdom of men, and gives it to whomever He chooses."[22] The one who rules on earth is God's choice.

We see this in the life of King Saul. "God removed him and He raised up for them David as king."[23] "So Samuel said to him, 'The Lord has torn the kingdom of Israel from you today, and has given it to a neighbor of yours, who is better than you.'"[24] We see this in the life of Pharaoh. The Lord God of the Hebrews told Pharaoh, "Indeed for this purpose I have raised you up, that I may show My power in you."[25] The Apostle Paul quotes this verse in Romans 9:17, "The Scripture says to the Pharaoh, 'For this very purpose I have raised you up, that I may show My power in you.'" God raised up kings and queens and He throws them down.

An incredible event takes place in Chapter 2. A Jewish woman in exile becomes queen of the greatest empire in the world at that time. She is supernaturally selected from among tens of thousands of women in the Persian Empire. She is "Hadassah" or "Esther," and the Lord will use her to save His people from annihilation. Let us go now to Chapter 2 and see the results of the "Miss Persia Beauty Pageant."

---

[22] See Daniel 4:17 and 4:32.
[23] See Acts 13:22.
[24] See 1 Samuel 15:28. See also 1 Samuel 13:14 and 28:17.
[25] See Exodus 9:16.

THE BOOK OF ESTHER

2

Esther Made Queen

*"The king loved Esther more than all the other
women, and she obtained grace and favor in his
sight more than all the virgins; so he set the
royal crown upon her head and made her queen
instead of Vashti." (Esther 2:17)*

O ne of the most amazing things in this story is
the selection of Esther as queen in the Persian
Empire. It is one of the great miracles of the
Old Testament.

Some historians estimate that the Persian Empire had
around forty to fifty million people. For the sake of example,
let's suppose that there were 50,000,000 people in this
kingdom at the time of Esther. Suppose again that half of
this population are women, or 25,000,000. Again, just for
the sake of seeing this miracle, suppose that you eliminate
all the children, older women, married women, those who
are disabled, and ones that are simply undesirable or just not
beautiful enough. Suppose from these 25 million women, it
gets narrowed down to 50,000 eligible women. Let's also

suppose that from this group, only 5,000 are young and very attractive. There is no exaggeration in believing that a massive empire of 25 million women could have 5,000 beautiful ladies. If you do the math, the percentages are very small. The Jewish historian, Josephus, writing nearly 2,000 years ago, said that 400 ladies made the final cut. Is it not an incredible miracle that Esther could be the one lady that is finally chosen from such a large pool of women? Yes, this is a miracle indeed.

Furthermore, she was an adopted girl. "She had neither father nor mother" because "her father and mother died" (2:7). She was an orphan. Also, Jewish women were immediately disqualified from the pool of eligible women because they were considered "exiles" (2:6) or mere slaves in Persia (this is part of Esther's well-kept secret that allowed her to compete in this pageant).

We can safely say that the odds are "a million to one" that Esther – a Jewish orphan – would be selected queen from among so many women. This is God's providence at work. This is the favor of God going before Esther. Only God could allow and raise up a young lady like her to win this contest among so many beautiful girls. The Lord is a miracle worker. Nothing is impossible for Him.

Keep another important fact in mind: It took nearly four years to conduct this beauty/queen pageant. Remember that Vashti was removed in the "third year of his reign" (1:3) and Esther is finally chosen in "the month of Tebeth (January), in the seventh year of his reign" (2:16). "Officers" had to go to "all the provinces of his kingdom" to "gather all the beautiful young virgins to Shushan" (2:3). The Persian Empire was so vast that it covered two million square miles. To go to every city, town, and village and bring these "beautiful virgins" to the capital, was a massive undertaking. It took years. The beauty treatments alone took one year (2:12)!

As we saw in the first chapter, "the third year of his reign" was 483 B.C. We know from Herodotus, the Greek historian, that in 480 B.C., there were two major battles between the Persians and the Greeks. King Ahasuerus finally led a million-man[26] army against the Greeks. The Persians defeated a small army of 300 Spartans in the battle at Thermopylae, but saw all of their naval vessels destroyed in the battle at Salamis.

In summary, Vashti is removed in 483 B.C., the battles of Thermopylae and Salamis take place in 480 B.C., then the king comes home and waits patiently through "six months of oil of myrrh, and six months of perfumes and preparations for beautifying women" (2:12), so that puts us at 479 B.C. This is the "seventh year of his reign" (2:16). This is the year that Esther is chosen queen in Persia. This is a rough historical setting of Esther Chapter 2. Let's begin our commentary with Esther 2:1.

This verse reads: "After these things, when the wrath of King Ahasuerus subsided, he remembered Vashti, what she had done, and what had been decreed against her." The king finally cools off. His "wrath" subsides. The terrible offense of Chapter 1 appears to be behind him. In a moment of reflection and "remembering," he recalls what Vashti did and Memucan's decree against her. Because he had so many concubines at his disposal, I don't think he was necessarily lonely. What he needs is a queen. Verse 4 makes this obvious – "Then let the young woman who pleases the king be queen instead of Vashti." A replacement for Vashti is needed. This idea excites the king and he approves the plan.

Verses 2-3 give us the particulars of the "Miss Persia Beauty Pageant," as Chuck Swindoll calls it. "Then the

---

[26] These totals have been criticized by many historians over the years. No one can imagine how a king, who was struggling financially and who had to cover such distances, could feed and equip an army of this size.

king's servants who attended him said: 'Let beautiful young virgins be sought for the king; and let the king appoint officers in all the provinces of his kingdom, that they may gather all the beautiful young virgins to Shushan the citadel, into the women's quarters, under the custody of Hegai the king's eunuch, custodian of the women. And let beauty preparations be given them.'" This time it is not Memucan, but "the king's servants" who offer advice to the king.

There were three primary requirements for a potential candidate. First, she had to be "beautiful." Only the best-looking girls in a city, town, or village could qualify. Second, they had to be young. I'm assuming that the women had to be between the ages of about fifteen and twenty-five. She could not be an older woman. The face and body of women are most beautiful during these years. Finally, they had to be virgins. They had to be young ladies that had never known a man. So beautiful, young, and virgin were the only requirements for this king.

These young women had to be selected from all 127 "provinces in the kingdom" and they had to be brought to the capital city, Shushan, where the king lived. There was a dormitory, so to speak, called the "women's quarters," that housed all the beauty contestants. The king had a trusted advisor named Hegai who was in charge of this important operation. Hegai is mentioned four times[27] in Esther, all in this 2nd Chapter. We are told that he was "the king's eunuch" and "custodian of women," and all the beautiful girls had to come "under his custody." Of course, to have a man deal with very beautiful women from the great Persian empire, the king had to trust you and you had to be castrated! I know that sounds harsh, but the Hebrew word, "custodian," literally means "someone who is castrated." In fact, it is translated "eunuchs" in 2:21 and many other places in the Old Testament. It appears seven times as "eunuchs" in the

---

[27] See Esther 2:3, 2:8 (twice) and 2:15.

first chapter of the Book of Daniel. The KJV calls him the "king's chamberlain," which is an old Middle English word that means "an attendant of a sovereign or king in his bedchamber." The chamberlain takes care of things where the king lays down to sleep, in his bedchamber. So Hegai was the eunuch in charge of this beauty contest to get a queen for the king.

The main requirement for winning this contest was the king's pleasure. Whoever was chosen had to "please the king." This is the simple statement found in verse 4: "Then let the young woman who pleases the king be queen instead of Vashti. This thing pleased the king, and he did so."

In verses 5-6, we find the first mention of "Mordecai" in the Book of Esther.[28] We are told a lot about him in only two verses. "In Shushan the citadel there was a certain Jew whose name was Mordecai the son of Jair, the son of Shimei, the son of Kish, a Benjamite. Kish had been carried away from Jerusalem with the captives who had been captured with Jeconiah king of Judah, whom Nebuchadnezzar the king of Babylon had carried away." Mordecai is living in the capital, Shushan. He is already in the city where all the main scenes of the Book of Esther will take place.

Mordecai's Jewish identity will be the single most important aspect of his story in Esther. He was "a certain Jew." When asked why he wouldn't bow down to Haman in Chapter 3, he tells them it is because "he was a Jew" (3:4). After that, he is identified as "Mordecai the Jew" (5:13), "Mordecai the Jew" (6:10), "Mordecai the Jew" (8:7), "Mordecai the Jew" (9:29), and "Mordecai the Jew" (10:3). Jobes says, "When Mordecai is introduced in 2:5, he is identified not as a wise man or as an official in the court, but

---

[28] A "Mordecai" is also mentioned in Ezra 2:2 and Nehemiah 7:7. If this is the Mordecai of Esther, he returned from exile with Zerubbabel.

as a Jew of the tribe of Benjamin."[29] We will say much more about his Jewish identity in later chapters.

Right away, we notice a critical connection between Mordecai and "Kish, a Benjamite." In the next chapter, we will go into a lot of detail on this important point. In 1 Samuel 9:1, when the Bible introduces us to King Saul, it starts with "there was a man of Benjamin whose name was Kish." "There is an unmistakable correspondence between his introduction in 2:5 and that of Saul in 1 Samuel 9:1."[30] Jobes makes this key comment: "By introducing Mordecai as a Jew of the tribe of Benjamin, the story is firmly rooted in Jewish history."[31] Even though Mordecai is far away in exile in Shushan, the story is still about God's people, the Jews.

How did Mordecai end up so far from home? The exile. Twice we see "carried away" in 2:6. The Jews were carried away during the Babylonian exile. "Captives" were "captured" and taken when "Jeconiah" was the king of Judah and "Nebuchadnezzar" was ruling in Babylon.[32] Mordecai is a Jew in exile in the Persian Empire. This will be an important truth when we get to the end of the book and we find Mordecai exalted and ruling in Persia. The invisible God places a Jew in the highest position (besides the king) in the land. God raises people up and throws people down.

Just as there is only one Moses in the Bible, there is only one Esther. She appears only in this book named after her. Again, like Mordecai, we learn a lot about her in just one verse. Esther 2:7 reads, "And Mordecai had brought up Hadassah, that is, Esther, his uncle's daughter, for she had

---

[29] See Jobes, page 119.

[30] See Laniak, page 173.

[31] See Jobes, page 101.

[32] To resolve issues of dating here, refer to Laniak's commentary. He writes, "The problem with Mordecai's age in Esther 2:5 is resolved simply by reading the relative pronoun in that verse in relation to Kish, the great-grandfather of Mordecai." See Laniak, page 180.

neither father nor mother. The young woman was lovely and beautiful. When her father and mother died, Mordecai took her as his own daughter."

Mordecai had an uncle. His name was "Abihail." Verse 7 calls Esther, "his uncle's daughter." Esther 2:15 says, "Esther the daughter of Abihail the uncle of Mordecai." Also, Esther 9:29 reads, "Then Queen Esther, the daughter of Abihail..." Esther had "neither father nor mother" because "her father and mother died." Apparently, Mordecai adopted Esther and "took her as his own daughter."

Esther's Hebrew name was "Hadassah." It probably means "myrtle"[33] (tree). The meaning of the name has no bearing on the story. Everyone today knows "Hadassah" as "Esther." "Esther is the only person in the story with two names. Leland Ryken interprets this as the author's way of depicting Esther as a young woman trying to live in two worlds – the Jewish world in which she was raised and the opulent world of the Persian court into which she was thrust."[34] Furthermore, "By mentioning both her Hebrew and Babylonian names, the author is highlighting Esther as a woman with two identities, an issue that will be brought into sharp conflict later in the story."[35] The Hebrew orphan will become the Persian queen. This was all God's doing.

There's one more important feature of her life: "The young woman was lovely and beautiful." Baldwin comments, "The Hebrew is more specific, 'beautiful in form and lovely to look at.'"[36] Esther was a gorgeous woman. Vashti was also a "beauty" (1:11), but her character was no match for Esther's. Esther was beautiful, young, and a

---

[33] For example, the prophets, Isaiah and Zechariah, used "hadac" in Isaiah 41:19, 55:13, and Zechariah 1:8, 1:10, and 1:11, and translated it as "myrtle" trees. "Hadassah" is the feminine form of "hadac."
[34] See Jobes, page 97.
[35] Ibid, page 98.
[36] See Baldwin, page 66.

virgin.   Her lovely features, humble spirit, and noble character allowed her to win the Miss Persia beauty contest.

From verses 8-9, we understand that there were "many young women who gathered at Shushan the citadel," but there was one that caught the immediate attention of Hegai. Esther "pleased him" and "she obtained his favor." This is the first time that "favor" is mentioned in the Book of Esther, and it is always associated with Esther.[37] She did not win the contest on looks alone, although that was important; she won primarily because she had God's favor. Hegai gave her "beauty preparations" even beyond the "allowance" given to all the other young women. Also, verse 9 concludes, "Then seven choice maidservants were provided for her from the king's palace, and he moved her and her maidservants to the best place in the house of the women." Esther was the cream of the crop. She went to the top of the potential finalists. She was already in a position to move into "the king's palace." "What Esther wanted; Esther could get. She not only won the favor of those who had discovered her, but also the favor of Hegai, who had powerful influence in the palace. And he says, 'Whatever you want, you can have.' Think of that."[38]

Many commentators question whether Esther "was taken" (v8) willingly or reluctantly. First of all, every young lady was responding to "the king's command and decree" (v8). They really didn't have a choice. I agree with Baldwin's view: "It is impossible to know whether she went without reluctance. It is questionable whether any woman could exercise the right of choice in the face of a royal order."[39] I think the best insight is provided by Swindoll: "Just stop and think: Why would a young Jewess want to get involved in a plan that would force her to leave the only

---

[37] See Esther 2:9, 2:15, 2:17, 5:2, 5:8, 7:3, and 8:5. We'll say more about this later in the commentary.
[38] See Swindoll, page 44.
[39] See Baldwin, page 66.

family she had, under the guardianship of one she respected and loved, Mordecai? Why would she want to spend a year shut away in a harem, culminating in a night with a heathen king that might result in the possibility of intermarriage outside her race? No question, I think it's safe to say she went reluctantly."[40]

The king, Hegai, the king's eunuchs, the king's servants, the other contestants, and other men could look at Esther, but there was one thing that none of them could know. They were not allowed to know her identity. She was Jewish. If Hegai or anyone else had found out this truth, she would have been immediately disqualified. No Jewish exile could be a Persian queen.

Verse 10 states plainly, "Esther had not revealed her people or family, for Mordecai had charged her not to reveal it." In verse 20, again we have this secrecy: "Now Esther had not revealed her family and her people, just as Mordecai had charged her, for Esther obeyed the command of Mordecai as when she was brought up by him." Before and after she won, Esther's true Jewish identity was a state secret. Later on, this fact will add great suspense to the story.

Mordecai, with fatherly concern, checked up on Esther "every day" (v11). He wanted to know her "welfare" and "what was happening with her." He seemed to be restless and anxious. "Mordecai paced" back and forth "in front of the court of the women's quarters." I think maybe he feared that she would be exposed. Having a young lady talking regularly to a well-known Jew was surely a risk that could expose her true identity.

Verses 12-14 make most Christian women today cringe. Why would any woman subject herself to such degrading treatment at the hands of a heathen king? Laniak explains the dark situation: "After her single night with the king she would become an official concubine. This is clearly

---

[40] See Swindoll, page 43.

a sex contest as much as a beauty contest. The virgins were physically prepared and coached for a night with the king. They were encouraged to take something of their own choosing with them to the king, presumably something for erotic entertainment. The verb "to go to" (Hebrew, bv'), used four times in this short three-verse summary, has a double entendre – it is a common idiom for sexual relations."[41] So, those who failed in a night with the king, became one of his concubines, and was available to him only as needed. They went from Hegai to Shaashgaz. This was actually a miserable situation for most of these young girls, as they could no longer be married to a young man somewhere and have children. They were only there to gratify the king's urges.

It took "twelve months of preparation" just to spend one night with the king. In our day, if this was to take place, there would be such a political uproar, that any president or king would have to resign immediately. In that culture, the king was a law unto himself.

We are told that the women spent months "beautifying" themselves with "oil of myrrh" and "perfumes." They looked and smelled good. "She went in the evening" and "returned in the morning." You can only imagine what took place in the king's bed all night long. Each young virgin could take "whatever she desired to take." I'm sure it was whatever brought the king maximum pleasure. After "a night with the king," she was now one of the king's concubines, and rather than return to "Hegai," the woman would go to the "second house" (v14), "to the custody of Shaashgaz,[42] the king's eunuch who kept the concubines." The only way one of these concubines could return to the king's presence (or bed) was if "the king delighted in her and called for her by name."

---

[41] See Laniak, page 208.

[42] This is the only mention of Shaashgaz, by name, in the Book of Esther.

Hegai was specially trained and had inside knowledge of what pleased the king. He could advise each girl what would increase their chances of winning. Esther relied on Hegai's expertise and "requested nothing but what Hegai advised" (v15). He knew best, so she trusted his insights. Again, this all sounds a bit crude because of what is taking place, but Esther is using wisdom. Because of her beauty and wisdom, "Esther obtained favor in the sight of all who saw her" (not just Hegai and the king). She had favor everywhere. Again, we see God's invisible hand at work behind the scenes. The Lord was getting Esther ready to rule.

We are given the exact month and year of when "Esther was taken to King Ahasuerus, into his royal palace." It was January (Tebeth) "in the seventh year of his reign" (v16). The beauty/queen contest is over after Esther walked in. This is officially four years after Vashti was removed from office. Esther won because "the king loved Esther more than all the other women, and she obtained grace and favor in his sight more than all the virgins; so he set the royal crown upon her head and made her queen instead of Vashti"[43] (v17). After reviewing thousands of virgins, and "trying out" many, Esther is chosen queen. "Although her beauty was the reason she became part of the king's harem, she achieved all this without any of the advantages of aristocratic birth, well-placed friends, inherited wealth, or social prestige."[44] God is at work!

We should not try to read into this story anything about Esther's morals or being the wife of an uncircumcised Gentile king. That's not an important part of the story. God had to get a Jewish person in authority and power to prepare for the arrival of Haman in Chapter 3. God had people in

---

[43] This is the last mention of "Vashti" in the Book of Esther.
[44] See Terry Muck's comments in the General Editor's preface of Jobes' book, page 13.

place even before Haman comes on the world scene. Jehovah-Jireh provides in advance.

The fourth "feast" mentioned in Esther is called "the great feast" or "the Feast of Esther" (2:18). It was not just for Esther, but "for all the officials and servants." This feast turned into a national "holiday." This holiday went into effect in all the "provinces" and "gifts were given according to the generosity of a king." In Chapter 1, the king's generosity was seen in the "abundance of wine," but now it is with the "abundance of gifts."

Verse 19 says, "When virgins were gathered together a second time, Mordecai sat within the king's gate." This verse tells us two things.

Commentators often ask, when did the virgins gather the first time? No one seems to know nor can they determine the significance of such a statement. I have a simple explanation. The first gathering of "virgins" was in Esther 2:8 – "…many young women were gathered at Shushan the citadel." This gathering brought all the beautiful young virgins to the capital for the beauty/queen contest. The "second time" or the "second gathering" was to acknowledge and celebrate Esther's coronation as queen. Breneman writes, "Keil correctly maintains that it can only mean a second gathering of virgins after Esther was made queen."[45]

The second part of verse 19 provides more useful information. It says that "Mordecai sat within the king's gate." For years, as I would read through the Book of Esther, I thought Mordecai was a person who was unemployed and just sat near the palace at the king's gate keeping track of Esther's life. Get a job, Mordecai! Go to work!

After doing some detailed studies of Esther, I found out that "sitting at the king's gate" meant that Mordecai was a royal official or judge. He "sat" (like a judge) at the king's

---

[45] See Breneman, page 321.

gate to hear complaints and administer justice. "Throughout the Near East, law cases and official matters were handled near the gate area. Therefore, that Mordecai was 'sitting at the king's gate' suggests that he was an official of some sort."[46] Interestingly, it was while Mordecai "sat within the king's gate," that he heard the assassination plot of Teresh and Bigthan (2:21). Throughout the book, Mordecai is "sitting at the king's gate" (4:2, 4:6, 5:9, 5:13, 6:10 and 6:12). Mordecai was always busy serving next to the king's palace as a judge.

Next, we come to one of the key events in the whole book – the assassination plot against King Ahasuerus. In fact, the whole story of Esther turns on Mordecai's heroic deed in Esther 2:21-23. Ironically, in Chapter 3, Haman gets promoted instead of Mordecai, and in Chapter 6, Mordecai gets promoted instead of Haman. All of this was done by God's perfect timing.

The Assassination Plot

The Hebrew word, qatsaph, means "to burst in rage; to become enraged." It is used only two times in the Book of Esther. In 1:12, "The king was *furious*, and his anger burned within him" because Vashti refused his command; and here in 2:21, when "Bigthan and Teresh, doorkeepers, became *furious* and sought to lay hands on King Ahasuerus." Esther 6:2 repeats the information found here: "It was found written that Mordecai had told of Bigthana and Teresh, two of the king's eunuchs, the doorkeepers who had sought to lay hands on King Ahasuerus."

It was "*while* Mordecai sat within the king's gate," that he heard the anger and fury of these two eunuchs. It was while he was hearing the complaints of the people that he overheard the angry complaints of these two men. Almost

---

[46] Ibid, page 321.

nothing is known about these two officials except their names and that they were "doorkeepers." Literally in Hebrew, they "guarded or protected the door." Obviously, they were "secret service agents" assigned to protect the king and ensure his safety. They had immediate access to the palace and the king's quarters. We're not told what angered them, but their change of heart made them dangerous traitors.

Verse 22 reads, "So the matter became known to Mordecai, who told Queen Esther, and Esther informed the king in Mordecai's name." Mordecai learned about the assassination plot and he took immediate action. What if Bigthan and Teresh were going to commit the murder in the next few hours? There was no time to waste.

For the first time, we see the words, "Queen Esther."[47] And we see both Mordecai and Esther working together as loyal servants of the king. "This conspiracy is the basis for the first collaborative effort between the two Jewish heroes."[48] "She then told the king about it and gave Mordecai credit for the report."[49] Attributing the discovery of the plot to Mordecai is literally, "in his name."[50] This small detail will lead to Mordecai's honor in Chapter 6. It was the Lord Himself who placed Mordecai at just the right place at the right time so he could learn of this plot and expose it. The "revealer of secrets" made the secret known to Mordecai.

This chapter ends with the terrible deaths of Bigthan and Teresh. "And when an inquiry was made into the matter, it was confirmed, and both were hanged on a gallows; and it was written in the book of the chronicles in the presence of the king." Somehow the two men were investigated and it was "confirmed" and found that, yes, they were making

---

[47] This title appears fourteen times in this book.
[48] See Laniak, page 212.
[49] See the NLT translation.
[50] See Laniak's comments, page 212.

plans to kill the king. This was sensational news. Anything even remotely associated with an assassination of a king would bring the death penalty. There was no trial. There were no court proceedings. No lawyers were contacted. The two eunuchs were immediately "hanged on a gallows."[51] We will see this phrase again in the later chapters as Haman and his sons are hanged.

And now we're going to find a part of a sentence that is going to change forever the final outcome of everything in this book. One little phrase that makes all the difference in the world. The last part of verse 23 says, "...and it was written in the book of the chronicles in the presence of the king." The assassination plot and Mordecai's loyal deed were "written down" right "in the presence of the king." The king saw one of his many scribes write down what Mordecai did.

Something amazing happens next. Somehow, mysteriously, the king completely forgets to reward or honor Mordecai for saving his life. This was a big deal. This king's very life – the ruler over the vast Persian Empire; the most important man in the world at that time – is spared because Mordecai reports the plot to Queen Esther, who promptly reports it to the king. Jobes writes, "Acts of loyalty were usually rewarded immediately and generously by Persian kings, but Mordecai's reward was apparently overlooked."[52] How could the king not reward someone who just saved his life? *It was the invisible God, working behind the scenes, who made sure that Mordecai's honor was delayed until just the right time!* God always has perfect timing, and it was not the right time to honor him.

---

[51] The word, "gallows," is mentioned nine times in the Book of Esther, and nowhere else in the Bible. Stedman writes, "In the original Hebrew language, this phrase refers to being nailed to, or impaled upon, a tree or post" (page 38) and Laniak says that it "refers to the ancient custom of impalement, not the later Roman practice of crucifixion" (page 213).

[52] See Jobes, page 118.

What's amazing, as we will note in the next chapter, is that the next verse (3:1) has the king promoting Haman! The evil Haman gets honored and the righteous Mordecai goes back to the "king's gate." We must never forget that promotion comes not from the north, south, east, or west, but from God. He raises up; He puts down. It was not Mordecai's time yet. And, praise God, Mordecai is a humble servant of God because he makes no fuss over this terrible slight. Other people would have made an official protest over what happened.

Five years later, "in the twelfth year of King Ahasuerus" (3:7), the king remembers Mordecai on a sleepless night. "Then the king said, 'What honor or dignity has been bestowed on Mordecai for this?' And the king's servants who attended him said, 'Nothing has been done for him.'" "Nothing was done" because the time wasn't right. Now everything was right.

We should never worry about promotions at work or in the church. God knows everything, and He surely rewards His people at just the right time. The Bible says, "For God is not unjust to forget your work and labor of love which you have shown toward His name, in that you have ministered to the saints, and do minister."[53] God knows what you're doing for Him. He knows every sacrifice. He knows every deed done in secret in His name. So let us "serve wholeheartedly, as if you were serving the Lord, not men, because you know that the Lord will reward everyone for whatever good he does, whether he is slave or free."[54]

Let's us now go to one of the most painful chapters in the history of the Jewish people. Let's have a face to face encounter with Haman, the son of Hammedatha, the enemy of the Jews. He came up with a diabolical plan to

---

[53] See Hebrews 6:10.
[54] See Ephesians 6:7-8.

exterminate all the Jews everywhere. But let us never forgot – God is in control of everything, and He already has Esther and Mordecai in place to thwart and frustrate Haman's evil schemes. "There is no wisdom, no insight, no plan that can succeed against the Lord."[55]

---

[55] See Proverbs 21:30, NIV.

THE BOOK OF ESTHER

3

Haman's Plot – The Destruction of the Jews

"Haman sought to destroy all the Jews who
were throughout the whole kingdom of
Ahasuerus – the people of Mordecai."
(Esther 3:6)

Let's first provide some critical background
information to this third chapter of Esther that
will reveal some powerful insights.

This is a hard truth to accept – *God hated Esau.*
Malachi 1:3 clearly states: "Esau I have hated, and laid waste
his mountains and his heritage for the jackals of the
wilderness." God also hated his descendants as the next
verse makes plain: "They are the people against whom the
Lord will have indignation forever." "Indignation" means
an aroused anger against someone or something. God would
be angry against them forever!

In Romans 9:13, Paul quotes from this verse in
Malachi and declares again, "As it is written, 'Jacob I have

loved, but Esau I have hated.'" Paul, as if anticipating an angry response to such a declaration, says in the next three verses, "What shall we say then? Is there unrighteousness with God? Certainly not! For He says to Moses, 'I will have mercy on whomever I will have mercy, and I will have compassion on whomever I will have compassion.' So then it is not of him who wills, nor of him who runs, but of God who shows mercy." God hated Esau and his descendants, and there is no unrighteousness in that truth.

Through his Hittite wife, Adah, Esau had a firstborn son named, "Eliphaz." Eliphaz had five sons through his wife, and one final son through a concubine named Timna. This last son was named Amalek.[56] Esau's grandson was the father of the Amalekites who became the sworn enemies of the Jewish people.

God hated the Amalekites because He hated Esau. The first enemy that Israel fought when they left Egyptian bondage was the Amalekites. As Moses was "on top of the hill" with Aaron and Hur on his sides holding up his hands, Joshua and his army were fighting against them. Notice these fearful words from Exodus 17:13-16: "So Joshua defeated Amalek and his people *with the edge of the sword.* Then the Lord said to Moses, 'Write this for a memorial in the book and recount it in the hearing of Joshua, that *I will utterly blot out the remembrance of Amalek from under heaven.'* And Moses built an altar and called its name, The-Lord-Is-My-Banner (Jehovah-Nissi); for he said, 'Because the Lord has sworn: *The Lord will have war with Amalek from generation to generation* (italics mine).'" God didn't even want Amalek's name remembered here on earth. The Lord and His people would be "at war" with Amalek year after year until they were exterminated.

Nearly forty year later, at the end of the wilderness journey, Moses remembers this event of Exodus 17 –

---

[56] See Genesis 36:4, 10-12, 15; 1 Chronicles 1:36.

"Remember what Amalek did to you on the way as you were coming out of Egypt, how he met you on the way and attacked your rear ranks, all the stragglers at your rear, when you were tired and weary; and he did not fear God. Therefore it shall be, when the Lord your God has given you rest from your enemies all around, in the land which the Lord your God is giving you to possess as an inheritance, that you will blot out the remembrance of Amalek from under heaven. You shall not forget."[57] Remember. Don't forget. "Blot out the remembrance of Amalek from under heaven." The Lord wanted them wiped out so that no one would remember them. These people did not fear God. They attacked Israel's weak point – where the weak, elderly, infirmed, children, and nursing mothers were walking. They were cowards. They attacked the most vulnerable of God's people.

Hundreds of years later, when Saul was king over Israel, the prophet Samuel remembered again what Amalek did. "Samuel also said to Saul, 'The Lord sent me to anoint you king over His people, over Israel. Now therefore, heed the voice of the words of the Lord. Thus says the Lord of hosts: 'I will punish Amalek for what he did to Israel, how he ambushed him on the way when he came up from Egypt. Now go and attack Amalek, and utterly destroy all that they have, and do not spare them. But kill both man and woman, infant and nursing child, ox and sheep, camel and donkey.'"[58] Don't spare them. Utterly consume them. Totally destroy them. These were King Saul's marching orders.

Because Saul and his men disobeyed this command, the Lord was deeply grieved. "I greatly regret that I have set up Saul as king, for he has turned back from following Me, and has not performed My commandments," the Lord said.

---

[57] See Deuteronomy 25:17-19.
[58] See 1 Samuel 15:1-3.

It also upset the prophet: "And it grieved Samuel, and he cried out to the Lord all night." After Saul's disobedience, Samuel told him, "The Lord sent you on a mission, and said, 'Go, and utterly destroy the sinners, the Amalekites, and fight against them until they are consumed.'"[59] God wanted them all consumed and destroyed.

When all was said and done, the prophet Samuel unleashed God's wrath and fury. He held nothing back. Saul had spared the king of the Amalekites, Agag. Samuel spared nothing. "But Samuel said to Agag, 'As your sword has made women childless, so shall your mother be childless among women.' And Samuel hacked Agag in pieces before the Lord in Gilgal." It is difficult to see a holy man of God swinging a deadly sword with full force – "before the Lord" – and dismembering Agag. He "hacked him in pieces." It was a very bloody scene. Blood was everywhere. Samuel was probably covered in blood. Agag's body parts – arms, legs, fingers, head, and torso – were thrown all over the ground. Such was the wrath of God against the Amalekites.

Later on, when Saul consulted the witch at Endor, and Samuel's spirit was brought back from the dead, Samuel told Saul why he would not hear anything from the Lord: "Because you did not obey the voice of the Lord nor *execute His fierce wrath upon Amalek*, therefore the Lord has done this thing to you this day."[60]

Sadly, because Saul did not obey the Lord's command, in the end, an Amalekite finished him off while he was in the throes of death. This Amalekite stood over Saul and struck him dead with a sword. When he brought Saul's crown and bracelet to David, the Bible says, "'I am the son of an alien, an Amalekite.' So David said to him, 'How was it you were not afraid to put forth your hand to destroy the Lord's anointed?' Then David called one of the

---

[59] See 1 Samuel 15:11 and 15:18.
[60] See 1 Samuel 28:18.

young men and said, 'Go near, and execute him!' And he struck him so that he died. So David said to him, 'Your blood is on your own head, for your own mouth has testified against you, saying, 'I have killed the Lord's anointed.'"[61] All of this took place "when David had returned from the slaughter of the Amalekites."[62] Numbers 24:20 is right: "Then Balaam looked over toward the people of Amalek and delivered this oracle: 'Amalek was the greatest of nations, but its destiny is destruction!'"

You might ask, why bring up these dark and disturbing truths about Esau, Agag, and the Amalekites? *Because Haman, the great antagonist in the story of Esther, was an Amalekite.* Five times in the Book of Esther, we find the words, "Haman, the son of Hammedatha the Agagite."[63] Agag was the king of the Amalekites; Haman, an Agagite, was "the enemy of the Jews" (3:10). A great spiritual and physical battle was once again unleashed in Esther Chapter 3. Nearly a thousand years removed from Exodus 17, we have an Amalekite at war against a Jew. It was because "Mordecai had told them that he was a Jew" and he refused to bow that "Haman sought to destroy all the Jews who were throughout the whole kingdom of Ahasuerus – the people of Mordecai."[64]

With this important understanding, let us now look at one of the darkest chapters in the history of the Jews.

Esther 3:1 reads, "After these things King Ahasuerus promoted Haman, the son of Hammedatha the Agagite, and advanced him and set his seat above all the princes who were with him." This is the first appearance of Haman in the Bible. Out of nowhere, Haman the Agagite appears at a most unusual place. "The author places the promotion of Haman

---

[61] See 2 Samuel 1:13-16.
[62] See 2 Samuel 1:1.
[63] See Esther 3:1, 3:10, 8:3, 8:5, and 9:24.
[64] See Esther 3:4 and 3:6.

just where original readers would have expected a report of Mordecai's reward."[65] Swindoll comments, "Now, wait a minute! What's going on here? Mordecai's the one who saved the king's life. Right? Mordecai's the one who told Esther, who then told the king. Mordecai's the one who uncovered the plot and saved the king's life. So why is Haman getting the promotion?"[66] These are good questions. But again, divine providence is at work. The king completely forgot to promote Mordecai for exposing the assassination plot in the three verses just before this one. The Lord insured that this delayed honor would be remembered in Chapter 6 when the king has a sleepless night. The timing was just not right for Mordecai's promotion.

This verse starts out with "after these things." As we wrote in the Introduction, if we compare Esther 2:16 with Esther 3:7, there is a difference of over four years between Chapter 2 and Chapter 3. "The tenth month, which is the month of Tebeth, in the seventh year of his reign" is January of 479 B.C. "In the first month, which is Nisan, in the twelfth year of King Ahasuerus" is March of 474 B.C.[67] So between Esther's promotion to queen and Haman's promotion to prince, it is four years and two months. Based on the king's years in power – the "third year" (1:3), "seventh year" (2:16), and the "twelfth year" (3:7) – nine to ten years of time transpired from Chapter 1 to Chapter 3. I always used to read Esther as if these first chapters took place over a few months.

Haman is "giddal" (literally, "to make great") or "promoted." He is "advanced" and "set above all" the princes. They must have been the seven princes of 1:14.

---

[65] See Jobes, page 118.

[66] See Swindoll, page 62.

[67] The Jewish calendar started in March, so Tebeth was only two months removed from 478 B.C. Thus, four years and two months is the actual time between Chapter 2 and Chapter 3.

"Those closest to him (the king) being Carshena, Shethar, Admatha, Tarshish, Meres, Marsena, and Memucan, the seven princes of Persia and Media, who had access to the king's presence, and who ranked highest in the kingdom." Now Haman would out-rank them all. Later, this promotion would become part of his great boast: "Haman told them everything in which the king had promoted him, and how he had advanced him above the officials and servants of the king" (5:11).

Once again, critical to the story, he's an Agagite, the classic enemy of the Jews. Agagites were Amalekites. After the plot is revealed, Haman will be known as "the enemy of the Jews."[68]

Verse 2 says, "And all the king's servants who were within the king's gate bowed and paid homage to Haman, for so the king had commanded concerning him. But Mordecai would not bow or pay homage." Baldwin observes, "There seems to have been a general lack of respect for this man, otherwise there should have been no need for a royal command that people should bow down to him."[69] "Herodotus (the Greek historian) reports that such bowing was done extensively in the Persian court, since it marked social ranking."[70] "Bowing" was very common, but Haman demanded "homage" or "reverence" (3:2 (twice) and 3:5). Interestingly, "paid homage" or "reverence" is used in nearly 170 verses of the Old Testament to worship the Lord or false gods. Haman was definitely wanting people's worship not just a courteous act of bowing to one in authority.

It is important to note that "the king had commanded" this action "concerning him." In verse 3, "Then the king's servants who were within the king's gate

---

[68] See Esther 3:10, 8:1, 9:10, and 9:24. Compare also with 7:6.
[69] See Baldwin, page 72.
[70] See Laniak, page 215.

said to Mordecai, 'Why do you transgress the *king's command?*'" In the eyes of others, Mordecai was rebelling against the king. The peer pressure on Mordecai was enormous because "they spoke to him daily and he would not listen to them" (v4). When these servants could no longer take any more of Mordecai's disobedience, "They told it to Haman, to see whether Mordecai's words would stand; for Mordecai had told them that he was a Jew" (v4). Laniak is right: "The narrator makes it clear that ethnicity is the basis for Mordecai's refusal. Mordecai has explained his behavior in terms of his Jewishness."[71] "'He had told them he was a Jew,' which tends to support the argument that Mordecai had religious reasons for not bowing down to Haman."[72] The 2nd Commandment said, in part, "You shall not bow down to them nor serve them. For I, the Lord your God, am a jealous God."[73] I think Haman wanted Mordecai to bow down and worship him *because Mordecai was a Jew*. From Esther 3:8, it certainly appears that Haman knew enough about Jews, their faith, and "laws" to know that they worshipped the God of Israel and not the gods of the nations. In other words, not only did the arrogant Haman want homage, he wanted to provoke Mordecai to disobedience.

The fifth verse – perhaps one of the most significant verses in the whole story of Esther – reads, "When Haman saw that Mordecai did not bow or pay him homage, Haman was filled with wrath." Proud men are easily angered. Haman was "filled with wrath." The Hebrew word, "chemah," is variously translated as "enraged," "very angry," and "filled with rage." It's a word that means "heat" or "to be hot from a fever." Interestingly, it is translated in many Old Testament verses as "poison" (of a serpent) or "fury." "Furious" would be a good core definition. The

---

[71] See Laniak, pages 215-216.
[72] See Breneman, page 327.
[73] See Exodus 20:5.

same Hebrew word is used in Esther 5:9: "So Haman went out that day joyful and with a glad heart; but when Haman saw Mordecai in the king's gate, and that he did not stand or tremble before him, he was *filled with indignation* against Mordecai." Mordecai did not "bow down" nor "stand up"; he would not "tremble before him" nor "pay him homage." Haman was filled with wrath and filled with indignation against Mordecai.

I believe that Mordecai's refusal to bow down and reverence Haman is one of the most critical lessons of the book. *Mordecai's identity determined his worship.* He would not pay homage to a man, regardless of his position, because he was a Jew. Mordecai worshipped Jehovah God alone. He would bow the knee to no one else. He suffered – no, all the Jews of the entire Persian empire suffered – because of his stand.

Everything about Mordecai's life revolved around his Jewishness. It was also what he imposed upon Esther as a secret in order for her to become queen (2:10, 2:20). When he is first introduced in the book of Esther, he is "a certain Jew whose name was Mordecai" (2:5). He is a "Benjamite." He is the "son of Kish," and one of the "captives carried away from Jerusalem" (2:6). Notice how his identity is highlighted everywhere – "Mordecai the Jew" (5:13), "Mordecai the Jew" (6:10), "Mordecai the Jew" (8:7), "Mordecai the Jew" (9:29), "Mordecai the Jew" (9:31), and "Mordecai the Jew" (10:3). The main reason that he gave the king's servants for not bowing down to Haman was because he "told them that he was a Jew" (3:4). Like the three Hebrew children in Babylon in Daniel 3, Mordecai resolutely refused to worship anyone else even if it meant being thrown in the fire.

I wish we Christians living in our day would have the same convictions. I wish we would not compromise our beliefs on the idolatrous altars of today's politically correct and bankrupt culture. Will we categorically reject homosexual marriages because we are Christians? Will we refuse the false prophets of our day, like Rob Bell, who espouse a heretical doctrine of universal salvation? Will we preach that there is a hell and millions go there every year because they have rejected Christ and His claims? Will we come out of our closets and live a godly life in Christ Jesus even if we suffer persecution? Mordecai has set a high standard for Christians today. He absolutely refused to compromise even though it risked the lives of all Jews everywhere.

"But he disdained to lay hands on Mordecai alone, for they had told him of the people of Mordecai. Instead, Haman sought to destroy all the Jews who were throughout the whole kingdom of Ahasuerus – the people of Mordecai." In this sixth verse, twice we see the phrase, "the people of Mordecai." Haman quickly escalates the wrath against Mordecai to wrath against "all the people of Mordecai." He doesn't want one man dead; he wants them all dead. He wants "to destroy all the Jews who were throughout the whole kingdom of Ahasuerus." "Destroy" is a very strong word. This was Haman's operative word. Haman wanted "a decree written that they be *destroyed*" (3:9). Haman promised "to pay into the king's treasuries to *destroy* the Jews" (4:7). When Esther finally told the king her request, she uttered these painful words: "For we have been sold, my people and I, to be *destroyed*, to be killed, and to be annihilated" (7:4). Haman wanted Jews destroyed. He wanted all Jews destroyed and annihilated. That satanic spirit that was on Adolf Hitler was first on Haman. When referring to the armistice that ended World War I, Hitler said, "We are going to destroy the Jews. They are not going to get away with what they did on November 9, 1918. The day of reckoning has come." The Holocaust – the extermination of European Jewry in the concentration camps – was "the final solution of the Jewish problem." Haman and Hitler wanted Jews destroyed.

Have you ever thought deeply about why the Jews have been the most persecuted and oppressed people in the history of the world? The people of Abraham, Moses, David, Daniel, and Paul have been slaughtered century after century. Why? In fact, *they are the people of God.* In his remarkable book, *The Anguish of the Jews*, Edward H. Flannery calls Anti-Semitism, "history's most durable hatred." He makes these profound declarations and asks these troubling questions – "As the historian of antisemitism looks back over the millennia of horrors he has recorded, an inescapable conclusion emerges. Other hatreds may have surpassed it in intensity for a historical moment, but all in their turn have assumed their proper place in the dustbin of history. What other hatred has endured centuries and survived a genocide of 6,000,000 of its victims...only to find itself still intact and rich in potential for many more years of life? The very magnitude of the record, seen as a whole, cries out for explanation. How did this amalgam of undying hatred and oppression come to be? What is it essentially? Who or what was responsible for it?"[74]

Pharaoh enslaved the Jews for four hundred years. "Antiochus IV Epiphanes (175-163) pillaged and slaughtered Jews. He entered the Holy of Holies and dedicated the Temple to Jupiter Olympus. The practice of the Mosaic Law was outlawed under pain of death."[75] Early church fathers like Cyprian, Hippolytus, and Origen were clearly against the Jews. Justin (100-165), who wrote *Dialogue with Trypho* (a Jewish rabbi), blamed all the troubles coming on Jews as God's wrath against them for the death of Jesus Christ. Many Christian writers took up this banner in the following centuries.

---

[74] *The Anguish of the Jews, Twenty-Three Centuries of Antisemitism,* Edward H. Flannery, Paulist Press, New York, New York, page 284.
[75] Ibid, page 13.

No "Christian" teacher or writer came against the Jews like John Chrysostom (344-407). Flannery says that he "stands without peer or parallel in the entire literature against Jews (adversus Judaeos)."[76] Chrysostom, revered in many Christians circles to this day for his outstanding teaching of Christian truths, blamed the Jews for the "odious assassination of Christ." Unfortunately, he taught that "God hates the Jews and always hated the Jews" and "it is the duty of Christians to hate the Jews."[77] In 1492, Ferdinand and Isabella, devote Catholics, expelled all Jews from Spain under penalty of death. Martin Luther, the great reformer, was a powerful anti-Semite. Hitler used much of his writings to arouse Germans against the Jews. Voltaire, the French philosopher of the Enlightenment, held Jews in utter contempt. The Russian czars enacted terrible pogroms[78] against Jews. The Bolsheviks butchered and tortured tens of thousands of Jews. Six million Jews perished in the Holocaust under the Nazis. And we've said nothing about the Crusades, the Ku Klux Klan, Arab hostility, and Islamic nations and terrorists. What about the black radicals like Malcolm X, Stokely Carmichael, Eldridge Cleaver, Louis Farrakhan, the Black Panthers and the Nation of Islam? All of them vilified Jews and preached vitriolic messages against them.

As I am writing these words, Robert Bowers used a Colt AR-15 semi-automatic rifle and three Glock .357 semi-automatic pistols to kill eleven Jews at the *Tree of Life* synagogue in Pittsburg, Pennsylvania. As he was killing these Jews, he was yelling, "All Jews must die!"

No Christian who loves God can hate the Jews. Flannery is correct: "The sin of antisemitism contains many sins, but in the end, it is a denial of Christian faith, a failure

---

[76] Ibid, page 50.

[77] Ibid, page 51.

[78] A "pogrom" is a Yiddish word that means "devastation." It is defined as an organized massacre of Jewish people (or any people).

of Christian hope, and a malady of Christian love."[79] Our motivation toward the Jewish people should be that of the apostle Paul: "Brothers, my heart's desire and prayer to God for the Israelites is that they may be saved."[80] Our hope for the Jews is "saved, not destroyed." Remember, Jesus was a Jew, the son and seed of Abraham and David.

Esther 3:7 tells us how the day was selected to exterminate all the Jews. "In the first month, which is the month of Nisan, in the twelfth year of King Ahasuerus, they cast Pur (that is, the lot), before Haman to determine the day and the month, until it fell on the twelfth month, which is the month of Adar." Jobes notes, "Casting of lots literally meant throwing the dice. But unlike their modern use, the ancient lot was used not for gambling but for divination."[81] "Pur" is simply an old Persian word meaning, "lot" or "dice." Notice carefully that it was not Haman, but "*they*" who cast the Pur. "They" were probably sorcerers (diviners) that worked with government officials like in Egypt and Babylon. Persians believed that the gods determined fate. They kept throwing the ancient dice until the evilest day was chosen. The day that the lot fell on was "the thirteenth day of the twelfth month, the month of Adar" (3:13, 8:12, 9:1). This was February 13th. The lot was cast "in the first month, which is the month of Nisan," or March.

From Haman's perspective, this plan was demonic. The Jews would be tormented for nearly one year as they thought about their total extermination. As Swindoll comments, "He not only wanted to kill them; he wanted to torture them."[82] Can you imagine how terrorizing it would be if they told you that in ninety days you will be hanged from a noose in the public square? You wouldn't sleep for ninety days. This was pure torture. Haman was probably

---

[79] Ibid, page 295.
[80] See Romans 10:1.
[81] See Jobes, page 122.
[82] See Swindoll, page 69.

licking his chops knowing that the Jews had eleven months to contemplate their complete annihilation. The dread and fear that this would bring upon them was horrific.

However, the book of Esther is not about Haman's victory, but God's providence. Everything is working toward His purposes. God oversaw the roll of the lot. Haman wanted torture; God wanted time. Think about it: if the dice had rolled and landed on a day to kill everyone in April or May, the Jews would have no time to defend themselves. But if the dice lands on Adar, or February, this would give the Jews plenty of time to arm themselves later – by Mordecai's decree (Esther 8) – and defend their own people. God made sure that the lot gave them all the time they needed to get ready. The Lord knew in advance that Haman's decree would be declared, and He also knew in advance that Haman would fall and Mordecai would essentially take his place. God knew that Mordecai's decree would take up to a few months to get to the furthest corners of the Persian Empire. Haman and his sorcerers had their plans, but God overrode them. "The Lord does whatever pleases Him, in the heavens and on the earth, in the seas and all their depths." "I make known the end from the beginning, from ancient times, what is still to come. I say: My purpose will stand, and I will do all that I please." "Our God is in heaven; He does whatever He pleases." "He does as He pleases with the powers of heaven and the peoples of the earth. No one can hold back His hand or say to Him: 'What have You done?'"[83]

There is something very deceptive about verses 8-11 – *Haman never mentions the "Jews" by name.* Notice the words that Haman uses: "a certain *people*," "*their* laws," "*they* did not keep," "not fitting to let *them* remain," and "that *they* be destroyed." Even the king says "the *people*" and "do with *them* as seems good to you." Again, there is

---

[83] See Psalm 135:6; Isaiah 46:10; Psalm 115:3; Daniel 4:35.

no mention of "the Jews." Perhaps the words written twice, "the people of Mordecai" and "the people of Mordecai," in verse 6 are given to alert us to Haman's underhanded ways in verse 8. "Haman carefully avoids mentioning that these people are the Jews, and the king is apparently too apathetic to ask which people are so charged."[84] Laniak makes this important observation: "Haman never explains that a personal feud with Mordecai is at the root of the plan. How ironic that he enlists the king's support to annihilate an ethnic group that includes a man who saved the king's life and a woman who shares the king's bed!"[85] There is no way that Haman would have mentioned Mordecai's name for fear of the king's wrath. Mordecai had saved the king's life in 2:21-23.

It seems to me that wherever evil things are happening, there will be lots of money involved. Esther 3:9 says, "If it pleases the king, let a decree be written that they be destroyed, and I will pay ten thousand talents of silver into the hands of those who do the work, to bring it into the king's treasuries." Taking a line from Queen Esther, Haman carefully words his request before the king – "If it pleases the king." The Persian Empire was a kingdom of laws and decrees, as we have already noted in the Introduction and first chapter, so Haman wants "everything in writing" – "Let a decree be written." The request is simple and deadly: "That they be destroyed." Persian laws and decrees signed with the king's signet ring could not be rescinded or altered. Haman wanted a guarantee of the destruction of the Jews.

Raul Hilberg, the Jewish political science professor, wrote the powerful and disturbing book, *The Destruction of the European Jews.* He systemically documents in page after page how the Nazis deliberately and willfully exterminated the Jewish people. The Nazis carefully built

---

[84] See Jobes, page 121.
[85] See Laniak, page 218.

concentration camps, a network of railways, employed thousands of their best people, and organized a very structured command of mass destruction. *And they used millions of German Reichsmarks to destroy millions of Jews.*

Haman wanted to pay everyone who would do this diabolical work – "I will pay ten thousand talents of silver *into the hands of those who do the work.*" This is 375 tons of silver. At the time of my writing this chapter, this amount of silver would be worth $170 million. How could one man amass such a great fortune? Well, either he would "plunder their (Jews') possessions" (3:13) or draw from "his great riches" (5:11). Mordecai would later tell Esther of "the sum of money that Haman had promised to pay into the king's treasuries to destroy the Jews" (4:7). Mordecai mentions nothing about Haman taking anything from the Jews to gather the "ten thousand talents." The king, having depleted most of his financial resources to fight foreign wars, was delighted that someone would give such an enormous amount "into the king's treasuries."

The decree was not drafted and then sent to the king for his signature. No, "the king took his signet ring from his hand and gave it to Haman" (v10). In verse 11, it reads, "And the king said to Haman, 'The money and the people are given to you, to do with them as seems good to you.'" Another translation reads, "The money and the people are both yours to do with as you see fit." *Do whatever you want with these people.* The most powerful ruler in the world at that time gives the most arrogant ruler complete control and oversight over the Jewish people. "That was his way of giving him unlimited authority."[86] The hungry fox would supervise the hen house. He was no ordinary fox but "the Agagite, the enemy of the Jews" (v10). This is the first time that the word "enemy" is used in Esther, but not the last time. Haman was "the enemy of the Jews" (8:1), "the enemy of

---

[86] See Breneman, page 330.

the Jews" (9:10), and "the enemy of *all* the Jews" (9:24). Esther identifies him to the king as "the adversary and enemy is this wicked Haman!" (7:6). Eugene Peterson notes, "Wherever there are a people of God, there are enemies of God."[87]

Esther 3:12 is a very long verse. It tells us many things. "Then the king's scribes were called on the thirteenth day of the first month, and a decree was written according to all that Haman commanded – to the king's satraps, to the governors who were over each province, to the officials of all people, to every province according to its script, and to every people in their language. In the name of King Ahasuerus it was written, and sealed with the king's signet ring." Although decrees were issued before this one, this is the first mention in Esther of "the king's scribes." They were called in "on the thirteenth day of the first month." This was Nisan 13th or March 13th. This was another demonic scheme of Haman – "according to all that Haman commanded." Why was March 13th such a bad day for the Jewish people? *This was the day just before the most sacred holiday on the Jewish calendar – Passover!* While the Jews were making preparations to celebrate Passover, Haman has scribes writing a decree to destroy them. The evil Haman is doing everything to make life miserable for God's chosen people. "Again the author provided information that adds to the artistry of the narrative by giving a date only a Jew would know. The fourteenth day was the first day of Passover, the celebration of deliverance from Egypt. The irony is unmistakable. The day before celebrating freedom from Egyptian oppression, a decree had been made for their very destruction."[88] Jobes writes, "The edict of death is sent (actually written) out on the thirteenth day of the first month,

---

[87] See Eugene Peterson, page 219, *Five Smooth Stones for Pastoral Work*.

[88] See Breneman, page 331.

which ironically is the very eve of Passover. The joy of the holiday is turned to sorrow in Persia when the decree is delivered on Passover."[89]

He also made sure that everyone knew about his dark desires – "to *each* province," "to officials of *all* people," "to *every* province," and "to *every* people in their language." No one was left out. Everyone would hear of Haman's decree. Breneman rightly calls the decree, the "death document."[90]

To deflect some of the ultimate responsibility away from him, Haman had the decree "written in the name of King Ahasuerus, and sealed with the king's signet ring." With the king's ring in his hand, Haman was now the most powerful man in Persia. Like Jeremiah, Job, Asaph (Psalm 73), and Habakkuk before us, we have to ask, why do the wicked prosper? Well, God has a plan. God would be at war with the Amalekites forever. Haman's downfall was secure. Let's keep Esther 8:2 in mind: "So the king took off his signet ring, which he had taken from Haman, and gave it to Mordecai." The tables will soon turn because God is in control. The signet ring will be on Mordecai's hand before the end of the year. *Patience is needed when God is at work.*

Notice the terrible wording of verse 13[91] – "To destroy, to kill, and to annihilate all the Jews, both young and old, little children and women" "IN ONE DAY." Again, this day was on February 13th or "the thirteenth day of the twelfth month, which is the month of Adar." Haman's "final solution" would be carried out quickly. No one would be spared, not even "little children and women." The personal feud between Haman and Mordecai had grown to a complete annihilation of all Jews everywhere. The "couriers," mentioned for the first time here and in 3:15, were literally,

---

[89] See Jobes, pages 122-123.
[90] Ibid, page 331.
[91] This verse opens with the words, "the letters." Esther will bring up these "letters" to the king when seeking to revoke Haman's decree in 8:5.

"swift runners" or "messengers." They normally rode "on horseback, on royal horses" (8:10, 8:15). Herodotus, the Greek historian, calculated that a courier would take ninety days from Sardis (in Asia Minor) to Susa.[92] Some places were 2,000 miles away from the capital. The Persian Empire was vast.

Haman not only wants all the Jews dead, he also wants "to plunder their possessions." This is something that the Jews will not do later with their enemies (9:9, 9:15, and 9:16).

Verse 14 says, "A copy of the document was to be issued as law in every province, being published for all people, that they should be ready for that day." Apparently, Haman wanted "all people" "ready" to attack and kill the Jews on "that day." The enemies of the Jews are never mentioned by name other than Haman and his sons. Perhaps Haman had a general uprising in mind. He wanted all people killing Jews. This "document" went "into every province," and "in every province where the king's command and decree arrived, there was great mourning among the Jews" (4:3).

While the Jews were mourning, the king and Haman sat down for a drink! "The couriers went out, hastened by the king's command; and the decree was proclaimed in Shushan the citadel. So the king and Haman sat down to drink, but the city of Shushan was perplexed." Such a cavalier attitude by the king and Haman only reveals the cold-hearted nature of both men. For now, "the city" and "the citadel" of "Shushan" were "perplexed." Pretty soon, it would be a place at war.

"Shushan the citadel" was the location of "the throne of King Ahasuerus' kingdom" (1:2) and "the court of the garden of the king's palace" where the seven-day feast was held (1:5) and where the king went to cool down (7:7-8).

---

[92] See Herodotus, History, 5, quoted by Breneman, page 332.

"All the beautiful young virgins gathered" (2:3) here to pick a queen over the Persian Empire. It was where Mordecai lived and worked at the king's gate (2:5). This is where Esther was selected as queen and taken to the king's palace (2:8, 2:16). Later, it is where both Haman's decree (3:15) and Mordecai's decree (8:14) were issued. "The Jews have killed and destroyed five hundred men in Shushan the citadel" (9:6, 9:11-12). Earlier, Daniel saw the powerful vision of the ram and goat by the River Ulai in Shushan (Daniel 8:1-2), and later, Nehemiah served King Artaxerxes as the king's cupbearer in this citadel (Nehemiah 1:1, 1:11).

For the next six chapters, "Shushan the citadel" will be the center of an intense struggle between Jew and Amalekite. Let us now go to the pivotal chapter of the book – Esther Chapter 4. Esther and Mordecai will work together to save the Jews by the invisible hand of God.

4

Esther's Call and Life Purpose

*"For if you remain completely silent at this time,
relief and deliverance will arise for the Jews
from another place, but you and your father's
house will perish. Yet who knows whether you
have come to the kingdom for such a time as
this?" (Esther 4:14)*

Why did God create man? What was His intention? What was His purpose? The famous Westminster Catechism written in 1646 and 1647 addresses these critical questions. The first question of this catechism states: What is the chief end of man? The answer is "man's chief end is to glorify God and enjoy Him forever." This is what God had in mind when He created man. We are creatures that should glorify God. We were made to enjoy Him forever. This is our purpose.

Purpose. What a simple, but powerful, word. Why did God raise up Pharaoh? "For this *purpose* I have raised you up, that I may show My power in you, and that My name may be declared in all the earth."[93] Why did God send Jesus? "For this *purpose* the Son of God was manifested, that He might destroy the works of the devil."[94] Jesus was sent to destroy the devil's works. That was His purpose. Jesus Himself said, "I must preach the kingdom of God to the other cities also, because for this *purpose* I have been sent."[95] He also said, "Let us go into the next towns, that I may preach there also, because for this *purpose* I have come forth."[96] Jesus was sent to preach the gospel of the kingdom of God. As Jesus was preparing to go to the cross, He said, "Now My soul is troubled, and what shall I say? Father, save Me from this hour. But for this *purpose* I came to this hour."[97] When Peter spoke about the cross on the Day of Pentecost, he said that Jesus was "delivered by the determined *purpose* and foreknowledge of God," and the Jews "have taken Jesus by lawless hands, have crucified, and put Him to death."[98] The supremacy of Jesus over all is so great that Paul could write "of the eternal *purpose* which God accomplished in Christ Jesus our Lord."[99]

According to Scripture, one thing is absolutely clear about God's purpose – It will be done! Nothing and no one can stop God's intention and purpose for man and this world. In fact, God's purpose is so sure that He has determined in advance how it will all turn out! Isaiah 46:10 – "I make known the end from the beginning, from ancient times, what is still to come. I say: My *purpose* will stand, and I will do all that I please." The prophet Jeremiah declared, "For every *purpose* of the Lord shall be performed against Babylon, to make the land of Babylon a desolation without

---

[93] See Exodus 9:16 and Romans 9:17.

[94] See 1 John 3:8.

[95] See Luke 4:43.

[96] See Mark 1:38.

[97] See John 12:27.

[98] See Acts 2:23.

[99] See Ephesians 3:11.

inhabitant."[100] Even the very kings of the earth, "God has put it into their hearts to fulfill His *purpose*, to be of one mind, and to give their kingdom to the beast, until the words of God are fulfilled."[101] When describing the eternal call on Christians, Paul said that God "has saved us and called us with a holy calling, not according to our works, but according to His own *purpose* and grace which was given to us in Christ Jesus before time began."[102] This all happened *before time began*. God's foreknowledge is beyond comprehension. When Herod, Pontius Pilate, the Gentiles, and the people of Israel "gathered together" to oppose and persecute Jesus to death, Acts 4:28 says that this opposition arose "to do whatever Your hand and Your *purpose* determined before to be done." God determined all of this in advance or "before it was done." The Lord talked about this opposition back in Psalm 2:1-2, over 1,000 years before it actually happened.

Nearly all Christians can quote the famous verse from Romans 8:28: "And we know that all things work together for good to those who love God, to those who are the called according to His *purpose*." In Esther, Chapter 4, we see why God raised up Esther. We see the eternal purpose of God for her life. She was "called according to His purpose." Esther "came to the kingdom for such a time as this" (4:14).

The 4th Chapter of Esther was a chapter of great mourning and sadness. In the end, Esther, Mordecai, and the Jews made a decision that would determine their destiny forever. Esther steps from an isolated position in the Persian Empire to the eternal purpose of God for her life and that of all Jews everywhere. Let's look carefully at this chapter verse-by-verse.

---

[100] See Jeremiah 51:29.
[101] See Revelation 17:17.
[102] See 2 Timothy 1:9.

The first verse starts out: "When Mordecai learned all that had happened, he tore his clothes and put on sackcloth and ashes, and went out into the midst of the city. He cried out with a loud and bitter cry." As typical of Jewish mourning, Mordecai and the Jews are "wailing," "fasting," "weeping," "crying," "in sackcloth and ashes," and "tearing clothes." Put yourself in Mordecai's shoes. Consider the depth of his realization: He was doing what was right. He was the only one in Shushan who refused to "bow down and pay homage." He was being an obedient Jew to the law of God. Mordecai would bow down to no one other than the Lord his God. His action was a powerful declaration of his commitment to Yahweh, the God of his fathers. And now, it is because of his righteous stand, that all the Jews are going to be exterminated!

It reminds me of when King David sinned by numbering Israel, and the Lord sent an angel against the nation and 70,000 people died. "David said to God, 'Was it not I who commanded the people to be numbered? I am the one who has sinned and done evil indeed; but these sheep, what have they done? Let Your hand, I pray, O Lord my God, be against me and my father's house, but not against Your people that they should be plagued.'"[103] David didn't want others to suffer because of his transgression (what a word this is for all spiritual leaders – even our private sins hurt those around us). But Mordecai's situation is perhaps more painful. He did not sin; he refused to compromise; and now, all the Jews in the entire Persian Empire will be destroyed by Mordecai's perceived lack of reverence toward the arrogant Haman. What a terrible feeling must have swept over his soul! He could be blamed for the annihilation of the Jews. Once again, the wicked appear to prosper and

---

[103] See 1 Chronicles 21:17.

the righteous suffer. The words, "He cried with a loud and bitter cry," stand out.[104]

"He went as far as the front of the king's gate, for no one might enter the king's gate clothed with sackcloth." This is all part of the phoniness of politics. To be in a state of mourning and sadness was seen as a direct reflection of how the king was ruling the kingdom. If people were sad, then the king must be doing a bad job. This type of message must never be communicated to a proud king. I recall how Nehemiah, the king's cupbearer, was sad in the presence of King Artaxerxes, the next Persian ruler.[105] He said he had "become dreadfully afraid" because he "had never been sad in his presence before" (2:1-3). Nehemiah almost lost his life because he "wept and mourned for many days" (1:4). No one did this in the presence of a Persian king.

This restriction on Mordecai introduces a suspenseful element to the story. Since he could not enter into the king's gate, how would he communicate what was happening to Esther? For Mordecai, a Jew, to be found talking to Esther out "in the city square" would raise suspicions about her and her nationality. Why is the queen talking to a Jew? This action could expose Esther to great danger. As we will see, Hathach will be raised up as a trusted go-between so that Esther's identity could be kept safe until just the right time.

In Esther 4:3, Haman's decree is called "the king's command" because it was signed with the king's signet ring. So even though this is Haman's dark scheme, it is given the full authority of the king of Persia. We will speak more about this in later chapters.

---

[104] Recall here the anguished words of Esau, when he realized that his brother, Jacob, stole his blessing and his father, Isaac, did not have another blessing for him: "He cried with an exceedingly great and bitter cry" (Genesis 27:34).

[105] Artaxerxes was the son of Ahasuerus. See Yamauchi, *Persia and the Bible*, Chapters 5 and 6.

Chapter 3 goes out of its way to express that Haman's evil desire and decree went everywhere in the kingdom – "throughout the whole kingdom of Ahasuerus" (v6), "in all the provinces" (v8), "each province," "all people," "every province," "every people" (v12), "all of the king's provinces" (v13), "in every province," and "all people" (v14). This "command and decree" causes all the Jews in all 127 provinces ("every province," v3) to "greatly mourn" and begin "fasting, weeping, and wailing; and many lay in sackcloth and ashes." Laniak writes, "While the citizens of Susa were bewildered over Haman's decree, the Jews were devastated."[106] While Haman and the king "sat down to drink" from their golden goblets of wine, the Jews are "weeping and wailing." Such is the way of rulers who feast sumptuously while their people starve. While his German armies were surrounded by Russian troops, trapped in the bitter winter weather of Russia, and destroyed by a lack of warm clothing, supplies, food, and arms, Hitler gave order after order for his generals to fight and never retreat. All the while, he sat in his comfortable heated bunker in Berlin playing war games on maps and sipping fine wines.

Haman despised Mordecai and the Jews, and he had not one ounce of feeling for the pain and suffering endured  by them. Verse 3 marks the bottom of the barrel in the story of Esther and the Jews. There appears to be no hope. "This verse is the low point in the narrative. Certain death was unavoidable except for the coming of a deliverer and liberator."[107]

Esther was so isolated that she was completely unaware of the decree. She was "deeply distressed," not by the decree, but "by Mordecai." Esther "sent garments to

---

[106] See Laniak, page 223.
[107] See Breneman, page 334.

clothe Mordecai and take his sackcloth away from him, but he would not accept them" (v4). She had no idea why Mordecai was mourning nor why he was dressed in sackcloth. She thought a simple change of clothes would change his disposition and allow him to come see her. Esther had to figure out a way to talk to Mordecai while he was in this state. God supernaturally provided a go-between.

"Hathach" appears only here in 4:5, 4:6, 4:9 and 4:10 and nowhere else in the book of Esther. The king had "appointed him to attend to her" (v5). He was "one of the king's eunuchs." He had to be a very trusted servant, and God used him to protect Esther. Esther "commanded him" to find out "what and why" Mordecai was in this state of mourning. "She did not go herself because her Jewish nationality was still a secret."[108] Hathach found Mordecai "in the city square" (v6). This must have been a very prominent place in the citadel of Shushan because later on, Haman parades Mordecai "on horseback through the city square" (6:9, 6:11) as he proclaimed his honor.

Mordecai then "told him (Hathach) all that had happened to him." Mordecai must have detailed how he refused to "bow or pay homage" and how this enraged Haman. Surely, he explained why Haman issued a decree against him and all the Jews. The main thing that he disclosed to Hathach was "the sum of money that Haman had promised to pay into the king's treasuries to destroy the Jews" (v7). Money was going to be used to destroy. The ten thousand talents of silver (3:9) were "a signal of the alarming scope of Haman's plan and the depth of his resolve."[109]

Just as important, Mordecai gives Hathach "a copy of the written decree for their destruction" (v8). Hathach was told to "show it to Esther, and explain it to her." These

---

[108] Ibid, page 335.
[109] See Laniak, page 226.

words let us know that the queen had no knowledge of Haman's decree. She was completely in the dark about what Haman was telling the king. This makes sense because "I myself have not been called to go in to the king these thirty days." The king had not called or seen Esther in a month. This adds tension and suspense to the story.

Everything was coming to a head. The powerful secret of Esther's true nationality would have to be made known. Verse 8 continues: "That Hathach might command her to go in to the king to make supplication to him and plead before him for her people." Mordecai commands Esther. Yes, she is the queen, but she is also his daughter. But this was not the time to talk about father-daughter relationships. The focus is "HER people." If the Jews were "her people," then she was a Jew. Laniak makes these important observations – "Now Mordecai was asking her to do something much more dangerous than keep her nationality secret; he was asking her to make it public," and "Mordecai makes Esther's relationship with her kin foundational to his command: He asks her to 'plead with Xerxes for HER people.'"[110] Breneman adds, "He was not exaggerating. Mordecai told Esther what to do; he urged her to go before the king and plead for her people. Now she would have to make known her Jewishness."[111] With verse 9, a heavy burden is placed squarely on Esther's shoulders: "So Hathach returned and told Esther the words of Mordecai."

There is immediate push back from Esther. She counters Mordecai's command with her own: "Then Esther spoke to Hathach, and gave him a command for Mordecai" (v10). She's not going to just stroll lightly into the king's office and ask for a favor. The startling truth is that if she obeys Mordecai as she did from her earliest days (2:20), she could be put to death. The painful reality of her Jewishness

---

[110] See Laniak, page 226.
[111] See Breneman, page 335.

is really beginning to set in. She was in danger if she went; she was in danger if she did nothing. If she went, she could be killed; if she did nothing, all the Jews could be killed. Truly, she had to make a life and death decision. Would she be willing to go to death that all the Jews might have life? "At first Esther apparently was more concerned about her own safety. But when she realized the influence she could have and perhaps God's purpose in putting her in her position 'for such a time as this,' she decided to act, committing herself to God."[112]

Verse 11 is a fearful verse: "All the king's servants and the people of the king's provinces know that any man or woman who goes into the inner court to the king, who has not been called, he has but one law: put all to death, except the one to whom the king holds out the golden scepter, that he may live. Yet I myself have not been called to go in to the king these thirty days." Amazingly, Haman had access to the king, but Esther, the wife and queen, had no such access. As we saw in Chapter 1, there were "eunuchs who served in the presence of King Ahasuerus" (1:10) and "those closest to him" "who had access to the king's presence" (1:14). Vashti was summoned, but she didn't come; Esther was not summoned, but she needed to go! However, there is a ray of hope with the words "except the one to whom the king holds out the golden scepter." But there's no guarantee that this would happen. Was the king upset with Esther? Did they have a fight? Were they not on speaking terms? We don't know, but "thirty days" is a long time for the king to be away from the queen.

Verse 12 adds an interesting pronoun – "So *they* told Mordecai Esther's words." After this verse, the following verses say "Mordecai told *them* to answer Esther" (v13) and

---

[112] See Breneman, page 338.

"then Esther told *them* to reply to Mordecai" (v15).[113] Baldwin notes, "Hathach no longer acts as sole messenger."[114] Apparently, other people besides Hathach are involved as messengers. We are not told who they are.

Mordecai pushes right back. He tells Esther, through the messengers, "Do not think in your heart that you will escape in the king's palace any more than all the other Jews." He is saying to her, "Just because you are the queen and 'in the king's palace' doesn't mean that you have an advantage over 'all the other Jews.'" Being queen is no guarantee that Esther will be spared. When it comes to being Jewish, no place is safe. All the doors around her will quickly close and she will not "escape." Essentially, Mordecai warns Esther that she will perish too. "In Mordecai's thinking, Esther's life may be in jeopardy if she goes to the king uninvited, but her doom is certain if she does not."[115]

Verse 14 is the most famous verse in Esther. Books have been written and movies have been made based on this one verse. "For if you remain completely silent at this time, relief and deliverance will arise for the Jews from another place, but you and your father's house will perish. Yet who knows whether you have come to the kingdom for such a time as this?" Note that the word, "time," is mentioned twice. Esther's "time" had arrived. The moment of decision is here. I recall the well-known words from Deuteronomy here – "See, I have set before you today life and good, death and evil…I call heaven and earth as witnesses today against you, that I have set before you life and death, blessing and cursing; therefore choose life, that both you and your descendants may live."[116] Her decision would mean "life or

---

[113] It should be noted that both "them's" in verses 13 and 15 are not in the original Hebrew but it makes sense in the context. "They" of verse 12 is definitely present in the original language.

[114] See Baldwin, page 79.

[115] See Jobes, page 134.

[116] See Deuteronomy 30:15, 19.

death" for her "descendants." What a weighty decision! "Mordecai points out that all of the previous circumstances of Esther's life that led her to the Persian throne may have been just for this moment when she can intercede for her people."[117] It is for this reason that she won the Miss Persia beauty pageant from among thousands of young ladies. God raised her up for this moment in Jewish and world history. "The outcome of Esther's decision is so far-reaching that without exaggeration she is at the moment when her life's purpose is at stake."[118]

Mordecai assures Esther that two things are going to happen if she "remains completely silent." One is good; one is bad. The good: "Relief and deliverance will arise for the Jews from another place." Again, God is not mentioned, but it is certainly understood that He is the One who is going to save the Jews "from another place." In other words, Esther is not God's only instrument. She is not the only option. God has other people He can use to deliver "the Jews." God is not limited. He has the entire universe at His disposal, and one person's lack of action or lack of faith is not going to limit His work. The bad: "But you and your father's house will perish." We know Esther's "father and mother had died" (2:7), but "Abihail's" family and the mother's family would all be killed. It was their "house" or all of their descendants who would die in the Persian holocaust. Anyone associated with Esther would die.

Just this past weekend, I was at my niece's birthday party. Her grandparents on her mother's side are all from Iran (former Persia). The grandfather's father was a very high-ranking government official in the last Shah of Iran's (1941-1979) government. When the Shah's government fell to make way for the Ayatollah Khomeini's Islamic revolution, anyone associated with the Shah was imprisoned

---

[117] See Jobes, page 134.
[118] See Baldwin, page 80.

or killed. This grandfather told me in his living room – with pictures of the Shah and his father on the bookshelves and walls – that he was arrested and thrown into prison even though he had no connection with the Shah or his father's politics. It was totally guilt by association. He was the son of a former secret service general. That's all the new governing authorities needed to know. He later escaped from prison and made it to the south of France and eventually ended up in the Pacific Northwest of the United States. He has lived in America since 1980.

Instead of death and dying, Mordecai appeals to her destiny. He calls out God's providence. Esther came to this position for just this purpose. She is God's liberator. *God's deliverer is already in the palace.* "Being liberator of her people was more important than being the queen of Persia."[119] Esther came to the realization, no matter how painful, that she was the only one in a position to deliver the Jews. God would use her to bring salvation and victory for His people. God could easily raise up another deliverer, but wasn't she the obvious choice? *The truth is no one else in the palace was Jewish.*

Mordecai asks, "Yet who knows?" Everyone knows. Everyone knows that Esther was raised up by God and made queen of Persia in place of Vashti so she could save the Jews from annihilation. She didn't choose God; God chose her. "Just beneath the surface of the story is another story. It's the story of how God works behind the scenes of our lives to accomplish His purposes."[120] Again, Esther is not just the queen of Persia; she's the deliverer of Israel! "The Lord raised up a deliverer for the children of Israel, who delivered them" is the often-repeated truth of the book of Judges. Yes, Esther is at the right place at the right time. She has "come to the kingdom for such a time as this."

---

[119] See Breneman, page 337.
[120] See Stedman, page 17.

In 2011, I was in a classroom with several other pastors and professors listening to Dr. Nzash Lumeya speak about going to the nations to preach the gospel. He was the president of the Fresno School of Mission where we all taught. "Who will answer the call?" he asked. He specifically said that church leaders in a remote part of Jamaica were praying to God for someone to come to them to help them train the people there in the Word of God. They needed help raising up other pastors who could care for God's flock. While Dr. Lumeya was speaking, an overwhelming conviction came over me that I needed to go. God was calling me. I was so captured by this call, that I actually walked out of the room and stood outside on the second-floor balcony.

I began arguing with the Lord (this is never wise):
"Why do you want me to go?"
"Who will go with me?"
"I don't have the time nor the money."
"What if no one wants to go with me?"
"Others are more qualified to go."
"I don't speak Jamaican!"[121]
"This will be a real inconvenience to my already busy schedule as a pastor."

And with many other questions and statements, I found myself running from God's call like Jonah. I even put a fleece before the Lord. I had an unwritten policy that I never travel anywhere away from home without my wife, children, or a friend.[122] I couldn't think of anyone who would want to go to Jamaica, but I thought maybe my daughter would be interested. She was a worship leader and could lead worship before I taught. She would be out of college during the summer and might have time.

---

[121] The national language in Jamaica is English.
[122] My wife could not go because she was taking care of her mother and my son was too young.

"Okay, I'll call Leah, and if she can't go, I'll accept that as a sign from You that I'm not supposed to go," I told the Lord. This kind of bargaining never works with God. Isn't that an outrageous contradiction: I was looking for a sign from God to not go where He wanted me to go?!

When I called my daughter to ask her if she'd be interested in going to Jamaica on a missions trip, she immediately said, "Yes! That would be so exciting to go to another country and minister to these people. I'd love to go! When are we going?"

My heart sank. Every excuse was being eliminated by the Lord. I had plenty of money to go. God provided the time and other resources. The only thing holding me back would be my disobedience.

Let me tell you the most critical part – all of those pastors and professors were very gifted and anointed to do many things for the Lord, but I was the only one with the unique skill set to minister to the people in Jamaica. I was the only one who knew how to set up Internet connections, laptops, projectors, and other technology. I was the only one who had extensive teaching materials on CDs and in written form with outlines and homework. I was the only one who had an open schedule for the summer of 2012 to speak at the Jamaican national conference. I was the only one who had served as a pastor for more than thirty years and had experience in raising up and training church leaders. I also was close personal friends with Dr. John Amstutz, a man who was a missionary in Jamaica back in the 1960s who started a seminary there that was still going. As I look back on it now, I was sticking out like a sore thumb. I was the glowing, flashing neon sign that stood out over everyone else. My whole life and training were for "such a time as this." By God's grace and mercy, I had been uniquely qualified to fulfill this Jamaican mission. Today, it is obvious to me why God called me and not someone else.

Unbeknownst to me, all these years, God was training me for "such a time as this."

At the time of this writing, I have now made six trips to Jamaica, and now many other churches and pastors have helped these brothers and sisters in their walk with the Lord. We are seeing the incredible fruit of a relationship with these Jamaican believers that only God could bring about. My daughter also received a call from God to minister to the poor and needy during this missions trip that still defines what she is doing today in ministry and her profession (as a school teacher). God is good!

Such was the case with Esther. No one else was qualified. No one else was in a position to do what she could do. No one had the connections with the king, Haman, Mordecai, and the Jews like she did. Esther was the obvious choice. This was her moment. This was her time. Thank God, she answered the call.

When we come to verse 16, we find no more push backs. Esther is determined. She resolved in her heart and mind to surrender herself to God's foreordained purpose. She is a woman of destiny. The powerful word, "go," is mentioned twice here. She commands Mordecai to "go." She also says, "I will go." "'I will go' marks Esther's momentous decision that risked her own life."[123] It's time to take action. She must take action if she is going to save lives. She cannot remain silent. She must go and she must speak. They must go and they must fast. Her steely determination is heard in the words: "And if I perish, I perish!" "She has changed from fear to abandonment and faith, from hesitation to confidence and determination, from concern for her own safety to concern for her people's survival. She has reached her own personal hour of decision and has not been found wanting."[124]

---

[123] See Breneman, page 337.
[124] See Swindoll, page 86.

Verse 16 starts with "Go, gather all the Jews who are present in Shushan, and fast for me; neither eat nor drink for three days, night or day." According to the next verse, verse 17, "Esther commanded him." This was an order, not from her daughter, but from the deliverer of the Jews! The queen is speaking with command authority. With three Hebrew imperative verbs of command, Esther tells Mordecai to "go!" "gather together!" and "fast!" She calls for three days of absolute[125] fasting with nothing to eat nor to drink. The only other absolute fast found in the Bible was done by the Ninevites after the prophet Jonah announced God's impending disaster against them.

This is important: Mordecai was commanded to "gather together all the Jews who are present in Shushan." These same Jews of Shushan will play an important role in defending the Jewish population in the capital on the thirteenth day of Adar in Esther Chapter 9 when Haman's "decree had to be executed" (9:1). These Jews who fasted ended up killing five hundred people (enemies) on the thirteenth and another three hundred on the fourteenth.[126] We are never told how many Jews there are, but we can estimate that there had to be at least several hundred Jews living in Shushan if they were able to kill a total of eight hundred people. In other words, hundreds of Jews were fasting for Esther. Of course, Mordecai led the fasting with these Jews.

---

[125] I would definitely warn against absolute fasts. What I mean is that it is dangerous to your physical health to fast from water for more than a few days. Every time I fast, I drink water. Also, although Moses was supernaturally sustained in the presence of God for "forty days and forty nights" without food or drink (Exodus 34:28; Deuteronomy 9:9; 9:18), this was never called a fast, but just a special time alone with God where He could give him the words of the covenant and the future direction of Israel.

[126] See Esther 9:6, 9:12, and 9:15.

Joining Mordecai and the Jews of Shushan in the three-day fast were Esther and her maids – "My maids and I will fast likewise." Esther had "seven choice maidservants" who lived with her "in the best place in the house of the women" (2:9). And it was "Esther's maids" (4:4) who informed her of the "great mourning" among Mordecai and the Jews. I'm assuming that these ladies were not Jews, nevertheless, Esther ordered them to fast. If she could command Mordecai to fast, then certainly she could command servants to do so. The power of God would be released when Mordecai, Esther, her maids, and maybe five hundred Jews in Shushan prayed and fasted. What is going to deliver them is not crying or mourning, but fasting.[127] All of these people will fast, but it is God who will intervene. I will say more about this in the next chapter.

At this point in the text, it is interesting to note that the word, "prayer," is not mentioned. In fact, "prayer" is not mentioned in any verse of the book of Esther. Normally, we see prayer accompanied by fasting. More importantly, "God" or "Lord" are also not mentioned. Why doesn't the author just go ahead and mention God? Obviously, they were not praying into the air. They were not fasting just to lose a few pounds of weight. They are praying and fasting to God. One commentator makes this insightful observation: "We are right to ask, 'If all of these allusions and coincidences point to the God of biblical history, why is He NOT named?' Perhaps it is not so much the PRESENCE of God but the HIDDENNESS of God in human events that the story articulates. To be hidden is to be present yet unseen. What is visible is only the human side of the story. Perceiving something beyond or behind takes faith."[128] Another says, "The complete absence of God from the text

---

[127] The words "fast" or "fasting" are mentioned only in 4:3, 4:16 (twice), and 9:31 of Esther.
[128] See Laniak, page 185.

is actually the genius of the book."[129] The Holy Spirit made sure the author left God out so believers could see the Lord at work through the eyes of faith. "As you read through the book of Esther, you will see that God is not absent. Invisible, yes; absent, no. His actions are on every page and in every line."[130] Finally, one Christian editor makes this perceptive remark: "Read correctly, the lead character of the book of Esther is not even Esther, but God."[131]

Before we end this study of Esther Chapter 4, I want to address a question that came up in Dr. Karen Jobes' commentary on Esther. It is an extremely important question, and we need to answer it accurately and biblically. She writes, "The modern understanding of divine providence has often seemed to dull, if not eliminate, the motivation for prayer. Divine providence is often misunderstood today as an almost fatalistic determinism. If God has already determined what must happen, then of what good is it to pray?"[132] This is a deep question.

Even though God is sovereign, we must be obedient. Even though God has determined the end from the beginning, we are co-laborers with Him. Even though the Lord does whatever He pleases, He uses human instruments to accomplish His will. Jobes answers her own question: "The story of Esther illustrates that human action is essential to divine providence."[133] Esther had to act or the Jews would perish. And if she did nothing, God would need to raise someone else. *Nevertheless, a human was needed.* "I planted, Apollos watered, but God gave the increase…for we are God's fellow workers."[134] There is no increase if we

---

[129] See Jobes, page 42.

[130] See Stedman, page 14.

[131] See Dr. Terry Muck's comments in the General Editor's Preface to Jobes' commentary, page 14.

[132] See Jobes, page 239.

[133] See Jobes, page 48.

[134] See 1 Corinthians 3:6, 9.

don't plant and water. "Surely the Lord God does nothing, unless He reveals His secret to His servants the prophets."[135] God could have kept Sodom and Gomorrah's destruction from Abraham, but He deliberately chose not to "hide from Abraham" what He was going to do. God could have scared Nineveh and its people into repentance by thunder and lightning, but He chose to send the prophet Jonah instead. The Lord could have killed Goliath with one small angel, but He anointed David and his slingshot. The Lord sent an angel to Cornelius who could have told him about salvation in Jesus, but He sent Peter instead. The Lord could have released the Israelites from Egyptian bondage without anyone's help, but He decided to send Moses (and Aaron). God could have prevented the seven years of famine from happening in Egypt, but He used Joseph as an interpreter of dreams and a deliverer of many nations. He sent Daniel as an interpreter of dreams and visions to Babylon. He raised up Solomon to give men wisdom. He sent Elijah and Jehu to throw down Baal worship in Israel. He sent Philip to the Ethiopian eunuch. He sent Samson to deliver Israel from the Philistines. He sent the apostle Paul to Antioch, Athens, and Rome. He gave John a vision on the island of Patmos. Most importantly, He sent His one and only Son to this world to die on a cruel cross and purchase salvation for all time for lost men and women.

God uses people! That famous word in Romans 10:14-15 clinches it – "How then shall they call on Him in whom they have not believed? And how shall they believe in Him of whom they have not heard? And how shall they hear without a preacher? And how shall they preach unless they are sent?" If God is so interested in saving the lost, why doesn't He do it Himself? No, He sends a preacher. He sends a person. He uses us.

---

[135] See Amos 3:7.

In one verse Jesus states, "For your Father knows the things you have need of before you ask Him." That sounds like we don't need to ask or worry about anything. Yet, in the very next verse, the Lord said, "Therefore, in this manner, pray!" *It is because God knows everything about our needs that we should give ourselves to pray directly to Him. Just because God knows doesn't mean we should not ask.* "Ask, and it will be given to you; seek, and you will find; knock, and it will be opened to you. For everyone who asks receives, and he who seeks finds, and to him who knocks it will be opened."[136]

I thank God that Esther acted. And when she acted, God delivered! John Quincy Adams once wrote, "Duty is ours, results are God's."

"So I will go to the king" (v16). Even though it is "against the law," Esther will go. This is the exciting adventure that we will look at in the next chapter.

---

[136] For the verses in this paragraph, see Matthew 6:8-9 and 7:7-8.

5

Esther's First Banquet

*"So it was, when the king saw Queen Esther
standing in the court, that she found favor in his
sight, and the king held out to Esther the golden
scepter that was in his hand. Then Esther went
near and touched the top of the scepter."*
(Esther 5:2)

The more you read the Book of Esther with carefulness, the more you begin to see key words, dates, and time references. When I first taught a class on Esther, I saw here in these middle chapters a key word: "Prepared." Notice how often it appears – "The banquet that I have *prepared* for him" (5:4), "the banquet that Esther had *prepared*" (5:5), "the banquet which I will *prepare* for them" (5:8), "the banquet that she *prepared*" (5:12), "the gallows that he had *prepared* for him" (6:4), "the banquet which Esther had *prepared*" (6:14), and "the gallows that he had *prepared* for Mordecai" (7:10). While Haman "prepared" the gallows to hang Mordecai, Esther "prepared" two banquets that led to Haman's hanging on the same gallows. Everyone's preparation eventually led to Haman's demise.

The first verse of Chapter 5 starts with "Now it happened on the third day…" We know this is the third day of the absolute fast of the two previous verses (4:16-17). Mordecai, Esther, her maids, and "all the Jews who are present in Shushan" (4:16) fasted. Perhaps hundreds of people were praying and fasting for three days. No doubt, God's power is released during these times of corporate fasts. The anointing, favor, and power of God came upon Esther over the next few chapters. We must not discount this important fact as we seek to understand what happened in these suspenseful chapters (5-7). The very person raised up by the devil to exterminate the Jews ends up hanging in front of his own house! Prayer and fasting turns tables.

Some of the greatest deliverances and victories in the Bible came from corporate fasts. This is a lost art today, but these fasts were powerfully used to bring about great triumphs. Consider these biblical examples:

After repeated defeats by a smaller army, the children of Israel fasted (Judges 20:26) and the next day they killed 25,000 Benjamites, nearly wiping out the entire tribe.

"A great multitude" of people from "Ammon, Moab, and Mount Seir" came to battle King Jehoshaphat and the people of Judah in 2 Chronicles 20. Jehoshaphat "set himself to seek the Lord and proclaimed a fast throughout all Judah."[137] Using a startling battle strategy, the king sent out the praise team to fight because they already had a prophecy that told them, "Do not be afraid nor dismayed because of this great multitude, for the battle is not yours, but God's."[138] God confused the foreign armies and the Ammonites and Moabites started attacking the people from Mount Seir and

---

[137] See 2 Chronicles 20:3.
[138] See 2 Chronicles 20:15. This word came through the prophet, Jahaziel, after the Spirit of the Lord came upon him. God begins to speak when people pray and fast.

killing them. When this was over, the Ammonites and Moabites attacked each other and killed everyone that was left. The Bible says tersely, "There were dead bodies fallen on the earth. No one had escaped." Indeed, they didn't have to fight for there was no one left to fight. They carried away so much spoils – "an abundance of valuables" and "precious jewelry" – that it took three days to remove it all. That place was named, "The Valley of Berachah" or "The Valley of Blessing." Fasting brings blessings.

The prophet Joel and the people of Judah participated in a corporate fast because of the ruined crops. This fast brought about repentance, restoration and revival. Because of their fasting, God promised that He was going to "pour out His Spirit on all flesh," and various people would "prophesy," "dream dreams," and "see visions." Everything that the locust had eaten would be "restored" and they would have "threshing floors full of wheat," "vats overflowing with new wine and oil," and they would "eat in plenty and be satisfied."[139]

The king of Nineveh and the people of Nineveh (along with the animals) proclaimed an absolute fast of no food or water to avert the judgment of God pronounced by the prophet Jonah. When "God saw their works, that they turned from their evil way; and God relented from the disaster that He had said He would bring upon them, and He did not do it." The fasting was part of the repentance that brought forth God's mercy. Fasting magnified the seriousness of the Ninevites before God.[140]

The early church leaders fasted in Acts 13 and the Holy Spirit spoke to them very specifically about who should go on the first missionary journey (Saul and

---

[139] For the fasts, see Joel 1:14, 2:12, and 2:16. For the outpouring of the Spirit, see Joel 2:28-29 (of course, quoted by Peter in Acts 2 on the Day of Pentecost). For the restoration of the harvests, see Joel 2:23-26.

[140] See this miraculous revival, repentance, and fasting in all ten verses of Jonah, Chapter 3.

Barnabas). The "Great Commission" Antioch church was launched out of a time of prayer and fasting.

Ezra and the returning exiles fasted to humble themselves and receive supernatural guidance and protection from God for the dangerous journey back to the homeland, and their request was granted.[141]

The prophet Samuel and the Israelites fasted after they had "sinned against the Lord," and this led to a powerful intervention by God against the Philistines whereby "the Lord thundered with a loud thunder upon the Philistines that day, and so confused them that they were overcome before Israel."[142]

David fasted to humble himself; Moses fasted twice for forty days without food and water while in the presence of God; Elijah and Jesus fasted forty days and nights; Nehemiah fasted after hearing of the ruins of the wall and gates of Jerusalem; Daniel fasted confessing the sins of God's people for their wickedness and rebellion; Paul was "in fastings often"; Anna "served God with fastings and prayers night and day"; Cornelius fasted and prayed and was visited by an angel; King Ahab humbled himself and averted immediate disaster by fasting; David fasted after God's judgment on his adulterous child.[143]

When His disciples wondered why they could not cast out a demon, Jesus taught that some deliverances only occur through "prayer and fasting."[144] The Lord also promised in the Sermon on the Mount that if we fast in

---

[141] See Ezra 8:21-23.

[142] See 1 Samuel 7:5-10.

[143] See Psalm 35:13; Exodus 34:28; Deuteronomy 9:9, 9:18; 1 Kings 19:8; Matthew 4:2; Luke 4:2; Nehemiah 1:4; Daniel 9:3; 2 Corinthians 6:5, 11:27; Luke 2:37; Acts 10:30; 1 Kings 21:27-29; and 2 Samuel 12:16-23.

[144] See Matthew 17:21 and Mark 9:29. Some translations eliminate these verses, but the Textus Receptus is correct and the commentaries of the early church fathers verify that it was in the original Greek manuscripts.

secret, "your Father who sees in secret will reward you openly." The prophet Isaiah, when describing the fast God has chosen, said it would "loose the bonds of wickedness, undo the heavy burdens, let the oppressed go free, and that you would break every yoke."[145]

People of God, prayer and "fasting" is one of the most powerful weapons in our spiritual arsenal! Over and over again, people in our church – and many churches everywhere – have used prayer and fasting to bring about spiritual breakthroughs. Many years ago, I asked a native Pakistani Pastor the secret of how the Lord uses him as an instrument to work many miracles and physical healings. His simple answer: "Prayer and fasting." Several recent books have been written confirming this wonderful truth.

Back to the matter at hand: When Esther and her fellow Jews prayed and fasted, it unleashed God's power and favor over their dangerous situation. It was no idle threat. God's people were going to be exterminated. Esther, Mordecai, and all the Jews in the entire Persian Empire were going to be killed. The three-day, absolute fast showed that they were trusting fully in the Lord and seeking Him for deliverance from a true holocaust. Esther moved out in powerful faith and incredible favor. And one of the most wicked men in the Bible, a man who sought to destroy the Jews, was destroyed himself.

As you read the Book of Esther, there is great suspense as the queen gets dressed in "royal robes" to "stand" before the most powerful man in the world. She had not been called in "thirty days." Anyone who came without being summoned was immediately put to death. Esther had lived as the wife of King Ahasuerus for more than four years, and he did not know she was a Jew. That secrecy alone adds tremendous pressure to the story.

---

[145] See Isaiah 58:6.

Queen Esther was so confident that the king would receive her and extend "the golden scepter" that she "prepared" a "banquet of wine" before she ever saw him. The Hebrew perfect tense verb for "prepared" (5:4, 5:5, 5:12) all indicate clearly that she already had the food and drinks on the table waiting for Haman and the king. There was no doubt about it in Esther's mind: The king would extend the scepter and receive his queen. That's faith. *Because she fasted, she had favor.* She didn't see faith, she saw life. She was bold and courageous.

Esther believed that she had received. Didn't Jesus say, "Whatever things you ask in prayer, believing, you will receive," "whatever things you ask when you pray, believe that you receive them, and you will have them," and "Again I say to you that if two of you agree on earth concerning anything that they ask, it will be done for them by My Father in heaven?" The apostle John wrote, "Whatever we ask we receive from Him, because we keep His commandments and do those things that are pleasing in His sight." Jesus said that the key was "if you have faith and do not doubt." Esther believed. She had no doubt. She received.

One commentator (Breneman), highlights the importance of the word "stood" in verse 1. "Esther put on her royal robes and *stood...*" The next verse says, "the king saw Queen Esther *standing* in the court." She was beautiful. She was regal. She had the anointing and power of God radiating from her presence.

Esther did not utter a word. That's amazing. Esther didn't barge in and make a scene. Esther didn't grovel on  the floor and plead for her life and the life of her people. She stood. The first reaction from the king is "she found favor in his sight." He immediately "held out to Esther the golden scepter that was in his hand." She asked no questions. She stood *and she was silent.* It was the king who asked the question in verse 3: "What do you wish, Queen Esther? What is your request? It shall be given to you – up to half the kingdom!" He offered a lot! The Persian Empire was one of the greatest empires of all time. It had 127 provinces stretching across the whole known world. To offer "up to half the kingdom" is an incredible statement. He wasn't kidding either. He exclaimed in 5:6 and 7:2 – "It shall be granted you. It shall be done!" Chuck Swindoll comments, "What can I do for you? Name it. There's no limit; it's yours!"[146]

Jobes says, "Vashti risked her life by refusing to appear before Xerxes when summoned (1:12). In another of the story's ironies, Esther now risks her life by appearing before the same king unsummoned."[147] Also, "The king knew that if Esther came like this, at risk of her life, she must have an important matter in mind."[148] She was wearing royal robes. She had not been summoned. She had even prepared a banquet in advance. Something is up her sleeve. What was it? Then the king asks again in verse 6, with perhaps greater insistence, "What is your petition? It shall be granted you. What is your request, up to half the kingdom? It shall be done!"

I believe the visible hand of the invisible God can be seen again. King Ahasuerus was a man with a violent temper. We know this is true from the Book of Esther and from secular histories like those written by Herodotus. We read words like "the king was furious, and his anger burned within him," "the king got up in a rage," and "the king's fury."[149] The first time the king asked Esther, she delayed matters by inviting him to her first banquet. The second time he asks, she invites him to a second banquet. This king is not a man to accept delays from people under his reign. I

---

[146] See Swindoll, page 101.
[147] See Jobes, page 144.
[148] See Breneman, page 339.
[149] See Esther 1:12, 7:7, and 7:10.

believe the Lord calmed this king down so that he would not fly off in a rage.

While God was calming the king, He was giving Esther discernment. She was given a blank check to ask whatever she wanted and still she would not make her petition and request known. This takes great patience and a keen discernment for God's perfect timing. Somehow Esther sensed that everything was not in place. Haman's arrogance had not come to full bloom. The gallows still had to be built. Esther's restraint far surpassed even Haman's angry restraint (5:10).

If there is one thing we learn about Esther in Chapters 5, 7, 8, and 9, it's that she knew how to talk to the king with wisdom and tact. Her famous lines – repeated throughout the text – were "if it pleases the king," "if I have found favor in the sight of the king, and if it pleases the king to grant my petition and fulfill my request," "if I have found favor in your sight, O king, and if it pleases the king," "if it pleases the king, and if I have found favor in his sight and the thing seems right to the king and I am pleasing in his eyes," and "if it pleases the king."[150] To some it may sound like too much flowery language, but I see God's hand on her speech. She spoke with great discretion and tact. She spoke with anointed respect, humility, and submission. There was no offense whatsoever. Does not Proverbs say, "Through patience a ruler can be persuaded, and a gentle tongue can break a bone?" One translation says, "soft speech." Another verse in Proverbs reads, "A soft answer turns away wrath, but a harsh word stirs up anger. The tongue of the wise uses knowledge rightly, but the mouth of fools pours forth

---

[150] See Esther 5:4, 5:8, 7:3, 8:5, and 9:13.

foolishness."[151] Esther used her tongue rightly, and "soft speech" turned the heart of the king.[152]

In verses 4 and 5, I want to reiterate that Esther had the banquet "prepared" before she went to see the king. "Come today to the banquet that I *have prepared* for him." "So the king and Haman went to the banquet that Esther *had prepared*." We're not told that both of them had to wait a few hours while Esther and her servants got things ready. No, in fact, the king said, "Bring Haman quickly" (v5). And even Haman tells his friends and his wife a few verses later that "Queen Esther invited no one but me to come in with the king to the banquet she *prepared*" (v12). All three occurrences have Hebrew perfect tense verbs that mean she did this in the past and it is affecting her present situation. Basically, she already prepared the banquet and had it waiting for them before she asked if they could come. Esther had strong faith!

Thus, in verse 3, the king asks what is "her petition and her request," and she invites them to the *first* "banquet of wine" in verse 4. At the first banquet, in verse 6, the king asks what is "her petition and her request," and she invites them to the *second* "banquet of wine" in verses 7-8. Esther has the king's favor, but he is exercising a lot of patience with his queen. Delays, delays, delays! *"Tomorrow* I will do as the king has said" (v8).

If anyone wonders why Esther delayed making her petition and request known to the king, Esther 5:9-14 give the plain answer. The gallows needed to be built, not for Mordecai, but for Haman. You get to see Haman's

---

[151] See Proverbs 25:15 in the NIV and NLT translations, and Proverbs 15:1-2.

[152] It reminds me of how Abigail spoke with such wisdom before an angry and revengeful King David who was on his way to slaughter her husband, Nabal, and his men. Her kindness and grace turned away David's wrath. Later, after the Lord struck Nabal dead, David married Abigail.

arrogance and haughtiness reach full maturity. The real
Haman comes forth in these verses. What Esther has been
waiting for has now arrived. Esther has waited on God, and
now God will act. I love that beautiful word in Isaiah 64:4,
"For since the beginning of the world, men have not heard
nor perceived by the ear, nor has the eye seen any God
besides You, *who acts for the one who waits for Him.*" The
world has never seen someone like our God. Let those words
sink in: God "acts for (on behalf of) the one who waits for
Him." Before you act, let the Lord act. Let Him fight the
battles; let Him work the miracles; let Him do the
supernatural. Stand still and see the salvation of the Lord!
Be still and know that I am God! Jeremiah said, "It is good
that one should hope and wait quietly for the salvation of the
Lord." Jacob declared, "I have waited for your salvation, O
Lord!" David wrote, "Salvation belongs to the Lord."[153]

As Esther waited on the Lord and His perfect timing,
Haman built the gallows, the king became sleepless in
Shushan, the servants went and pulled the scroll highlighting
Mordecai's heroic deed, and Haman inadvertently promoted
Mordecai and ate humble pie! *God acted because Esther
waited.* This is a valuable lesson from Esther's life.

When Haman left Esther's first banquet, he was on
cloud nine. He had "great riches," a beautiful wife, ten sons,
many friends, the king's favor, and a powerful position in
Persia. Verse 9 starts, "So Haman went out that day joyful
and with a glad heart." What he saw next, however, soured
his demeanor and "filled him with indignation." Previously,
"Haman saw that Mordecai did not bow or pay him homage,
so Haman was filled with wrath" (3:5). Now, "Haman saw
that Mordecai did not stand or tremble before him, so he was
filled with indignation" (v9). Mordecai would not bow, pay
homage, stand, or tremble. Knowing Haman's haughtiness,
we're amazed to see these words: "Nevertheless Haman

---

[153] See Lamentations 3:26; Genesis 49:18; Psalm 3:8.

restrained himself and went home" (v10). Haman's wrath and indignation have reached a boiling point. With the help of his wife and friends, he will bring an end to Mordecai's defiance.

Perhaps we could say that God performed another miracle here. With Haman's powerful position, and armed with the king's command that everyone bow down and pay him homage, why didn't Haman just arrest Mordecai and send him off to be executed? Perhaps Haman's restraint in Chapter 3 and here in Chapter 5 is the work of God in his heart.

Did you notice something different about Mordecai? In Esther 2:19 and 2:21, "Mordecai sat within the king's gate." After Haman's disastrous decree, Mordecai dressed in "sackcloth and ashes" (4:1) and "he went as far as the front of the king's gate, for no one might enter the king's gate clothed with sackcloth" (4:2). Hathach found Mordecai "in the city square that was in front of the king's gate" (4:7). Apparently, here in Esther 5:9, Mordecai has stopped mourning and removed his sackcloth because we see him once again "in the king's gate." In fact, Haman tells his friends and family, "I see Mordecai the Jew sitting at the king's gate" (5:13) and the king will tell Haman he can find Mordecai "who sits within the king's gate" (6:10). And, after being accidentally praised and honored by Haman, "Mordecai went back to the king's gate" (6:12). What am I trying to say? Mordecai had fasted and prayed. He had called out to God. Like Esther, he was walking by faith. He doesn't need to mourn anymore. God is going to answer the earnest and sincere prayers of these exiled Jews in Persia. He has done what he can do; now he is going to see what only God can do.

At verse 11, we reach the apex of Haman's pride and boasting. This vain man tells "his friends and his wife Zeresh" (v10) about "his great riches, the multitude of his children, everything in which the king had promoted him, and how he had advanced him above the officials and servants of the king" (v11). Baldwin points out, "His order of priorities puts his riches in first place, even before his sons."[154] Haman brags even further in verse 12: "Besides all this, Queen Esther invited no one but me to come in with the king to the banquet that she prepared; and tomorrow I am again invited by her, along with the king." "I'm the only one." "No one else is going." "Esther picked me because I'm the one who is great."

The great tragedy of Haman's life is that within 24 hours he will be dead; Mordecai will own "the house/estate of Haman" which includes his "great riches;" and Mordecai will take over the prime minister position he once held. Before the year is over, all ten of his sons will be hanging dead in front of his house!

The wisdom of God teaches us that "a man's pride will bring him low," "the Lord will destroy the house of the proud," and "everyone proud in heart is an abomination to the Lord – be sure of this: They will not go unpunished."[155] Of the seven things that God really hates (abominates), the first one is "a proud look" or "haughty eyes." "When pride comes, then comes shame." A verse that nearly all Bible-believing Christians associate with Haman is "pride goes before destruction, and a haughty spirit before a fall."[156] The "fear of the Lord is to hate evil," and that includes "pride and arrogance." As God's people, we are called to hate pride in our lives. Pride is the great destroyer. Pride always humiliates and shames the person who walks in it. Because of pride, Satan fell from heaven. Because of pride, Nebuchadnezzar ate grass like an animal. Because of pride, Pharoah's Egypt was destroyed. Because of pride, Uzziah was struck with leprosy. Because of pride, King Herod was

---

[154] See Baldwin, page 88.
[155] See Proverbs 29:23, 15:25, and 16:5.
[156] See Proverbs 6:16-17, 11:2, and 16:18.

smitten by angel of the Lord and eaten by worms. Because of pride, President Richard Nixon resigned the presidency. Because of pride, Hitler committed suicide and Nazi Germany was destroyed. Because of pride, Saddam Hussein, the once powerful dictator of Iraq, was found in a hole in the ground. God resists pride. One of the most powerful rulers in the history of the world once said, "Those who walk in pride, God is able to put down."[157]

I once knew a Christian man, a worship leader, who told me with a straight face, "I have the best marriage in our church." Within one year, he was divorced.

However, there was a kink in Haman's shining armor. Verse 13 reads, "But this is all worth nothing as long as I see Mordecai the Jew just sitting there at the king's gate." The NIV translation allows you to see the venom coming from his lips – "As long as I see *that Jew* Mordecai sitting at the king's gate." Like many people today, Haman hated the Jews, and he especially hated Mordecai. "The idea in our verse is that all his gains are outweighed by the one killjoy, Mordecai. In his present mood, Haman's irritation is becoming beyond endurance."[158] What happens next is going to give full vent to Haman's rage.

"His wife Zeresh" is found four times[159] in the Book of Esther, and she's first mentioned in Esther 5:10. She's always listed with "his friends." The ill-fated decision by "his wife Zeresh and his friends" in Esther 5:14 would have calamitous results for Haman's household. "'Let a gallows be made, fifty cubits high, and in the morning suggest to the king that Mordecai be hanged on it; then go merrily with the king to the

---

[157] See Daniel 4:37.
[158] See Baldwin, page 88.
[159] See Esther 5:10, 5:14, and twice in 6:13.

banquet.' And the thing pleased Haman; so he had the gallows made." If a man can "go happily" along and be pleased when someone is hanged, it goes to show just how sick Haman really was. Baldwin is right: "The connection between murder and merriment and Haman's pleasure is even more sinister than the gallows he had made."[160]

The word, "gallows," is found only here in the Book of Esther and it is mentioned nine times. Back in Esther 2:23, Bigthana and Teresh were hanged on a gallows for plotting to kill the king. Haman was hanged on the same gallows he built for Mordecai according to 7:9-10. King Ahasuerus said the real reason for his hanging was "because he tried to lay his hand on the Jews" (8:7). Another translation says, "because he tried to destroy the Jews.". So it was not only because he wanted Mordecai dead; he was hanged because he wanted all the Jews dead. Later, Esther asks the king to hang Haman's "ten sons" on this same gallows, and the king "commanded this to be done...and they hanged Haman's ten sons" (9:13-14). In fact, Haman and his ten sons were hung on it (9:25). And it all happened right in front of his house! Truly, "he who is hanged is accursed of God."[161]

Literally in Hebrew, it reads that the gallows were "fifty cubits high." A cubit was about eighteen inches. It 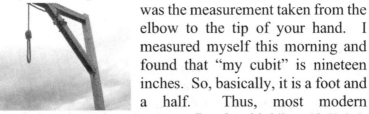 was the measurement taken from the elbow to the tip of your hand. I measured myself this morning and found that "my cubit" is nineteen inches. So, basically, it is a foot and a half. Thus, most modern translations have it as "seventy-five feet high" or 50 X 1.5. The width of Noah's ark was "fifty cubits."[162] A seventy-

---

[160] See Baldwin, page 88.
[161] See Deuteronomy 21:23.
[162] See Genesis 6:15.

five-foot gallows would have been seen from miles around, and apparently, word got out about this massive structure because Harbonah knew its height by the next day (7:9) – "the gallows, fifty cubits high..." I found it fascinating that in F. Murray Abraham's movie, *Esther*, when Haman clothed Mordecai in royal robes and led him through the city square proclaiming his honor, that they walked within seeing distance of these gallows. That was an ominous sign for Haman. It was certainly possible because of the enormous size. Jobes notes, "Haman builds a gallows of extraordinary size, seventy-five feet high, not realizing that its size is the measure of his own pride."[163]

Zeresh and his friends advised to do this hanging "in the morning." They saw how annoyed and enraged Haman had become. Why wait until the 13th day of the twelfth month (Adar)? Mordecai can be eliminated right away. As we'll see in the next chapter, Haman will not wait until morning. He comes over on the same night that the gallows are completed and the king cannot sleep. Esther 6:1 starts, "That night the king could not sleep." Verse 4 continues the narrative: "Haman had just entered the outer court of the king's palace to suggest that the king hang Mordecai on the gallows that he had prepared for him." Tonight! He could not wait another moment. Tomorrow morning was an eternity in Haman's eyes. His wife's evil plan "pleased" and "delighted" him. He could "then go happily with the king to the banquet." We can already foresee Haman licking his chops and offering a toast at Esther's "banquet of wine." Little did he know that it was all the beginning of his catastrophic fall from power. By tomorrow, he would be hanging from the gallows and Zeresh would be wailing in grief!

Laniak observes, "Haman has now twice concocted plans that will backfire on him. The date that was set to

---

[163] See Jobes, page 145.

witness the widespread destruction of the Jews will become the day for executing those who hate the Jews. This gallows, intended to single out Mordecai as first among those executed for *being* Jews, will make Haman first among those executed for *opposing* Jews."[164]

In the next chapter, we will see the visible hand of the invisible God. God will act. The Lord will do one miracle after another, all in a few verses. On to the king's sleepless night!

---

[164] See Laniak, page 235.

6

Mordecai's Honor

"So Haman took the robe and the horse,
arrayed Mordecai and led him on horseback
through the city square, and proclaimed before
him, 'Thus shall it be done to the man whom the
king delights to honor!'" (Esther 6:11)

No chapter in the Book of Esther magnifies the providence and the power of God like Esther Chapter 6. God caused the king to have a sleepless night in the palace; God caused one of the eunuchs to get the record of Mordecai's deed from thousands of records; God caused the king to honor Mordecai on the very night that Haman was building a gallows; God caused Haman to rush to the palace to seek to hang Mordecai; and God humbled Haman by having him parade Mordecai through the streets of the citadel. Is it not amazing that Mordecai does nothing and says nothing in a chapter where he is honored? God did it all. And Esther is only mentioned once in the last verse – Haman was brought "to the banquet which Esther had prepared" (6:14).

Sleepless in Seattle was a 1993 romantic comedy film starring Tom Hanks and Meg Ryan. *"Sleepless in Shushan"* would be an appropriate film title about the king in Esther Chapter 6. "That night the king could not sleep." As many commentators point out, it is literally, "the king's sleep fled away." "The Greek translation (Septuagint) makes this implicit truth with the statement, 'The Lord took sleep from the king that night.'"[165] The Lord made sure the king did not sleep that night. There was too much happening in Shushan for him to be asleep.

One way to help someone sleep is to hand him a boring book and start reading it. Verse 1 continues, "So one was commanded to bring the book of the records of the  chronicles; and they were read before the king." Let's not overlook this extraordinary miracle here in verses 1-2. Mordecai exposed a plot to assassinate the king "in the month of Tebeth (January), in the seventh year of his reign" (2:17). As we pointed out in chapter 2, the king completely forgot to honor Mordecai for his heroic deed even though "it was written in the book of the chronicles *in the presence of the king*" (2:23). Haman issues his monstrous decree "in the month of Nisan (April), in the twelfth year of King Ahasuerus" (3:7). So between chapter 2, when Mordecai saved the king's life, and chapter 6, where the king reads about his saving act, it is about four to five years later. How many government agreements, contracts, decrees, transactions, and historical events can take place and be recorded in the mighty Persian Empire in five years? No doubt, hundreds or perhaps thousands of records must have been written into "the chronicles." Historically, we know so much about the

---

[165] See Jobes, page 158. The Septuagint is the Greek version of the Jewish Scriptures translated in 3rd and 2nd Centuries B.C.

Persian Empire because there were so many "records" written down by the Persians and Greeks.

What are the chances of picking the one "book" that had Mordecai's deed from five years earlier? The eunuch who went to the "library of records" must have had hundreds and hundreds of scrolls to pick from. It was no coincidence that he picked just the right one. God made sure he selected the one that told of the assassination plot. Verse 2 says, "It was found written that Mordecai had told of Bigthana and Teresh, two of the king's eunuchs, the doorkeepers who had sought to lay hands on King Ahasuerus." This supernatural miracle also serves to heighten the miracle when the king did not honor Mordecai back in 2:23 so that it could wait for this exact night when Haman is building a gallows for him. God and God alone was the person responsible for this incredible timing and selection!

The truth is Mordecai was used by God not only to save the king (chapter 2), but later, to save the Jews (chapter 8), but more about that story when we get to that chapter.

Verse 3 reads, "Then the king said, 'What honor or dignity has been bestowed on Mordecai for this?' And the king's servants who attended him said, 'Nothing has been done for him.'" Talk about a bizarre situation. Haman is out there building a gallows so he can hang Mordecai, and meanwhile, in the palace, in the middle of the night, the king is trying to find a way to honor Mordecai. What irony!

The Hebrew word for "dignity" in this verse has already been used to speak of the king's "excellent *majesty*" and glorious kingdom in 1:4, but it will be used again in 10:2 of the "*greatness* of Mordecai." Surely, what Mordecai did for the king was the beginning of his "advancement" and promotion in the Persian kingdom. This was all arranged by God Himself since He is the One who raises people up or throws them down.

We are now going to see God's impeccable timing. Right after the king's first question, he asks another one – "Who is in the court?" Zeresh had told Haman "to suggest to the king that Mordecai be hanged" "in the morning" (5:14). Haman was so enraged with Mordecai's irreverence, that he wanted him hanged "in front of his house" (7:9) in the middle of "that night." Verse 4 continues, "Now Haman had just entered the outer court of the king's palace to suggest that the king hang Mordecai on the gallows that he had prepared for him." Haman just so happens to "enter the outer court" right at the moment that the king wants to honor Mordecai. Not only that, Haman is coming so Mordecai can be hanged; the king is waiting so Mordecai can be honored. The visible hand of the invisible God is at work!

Verse 5 says, "The king's servants said to him, 'Haman is there, standing in the court.' And the king said, 'Let him come in.'" Haman is there! He has arrived to honor Mordecai! He has arrived to make preparations for his hanging. No one – absolutely no one – but the Lord Himself could arrange this situation in the middle of the king's sleepless night. Truly, there is no need for Haman to request an audience with the king; the king lets him in! The Lord opened the door for Haman that would lead to his demise.

Observe again the providence of God that even the words the king spoke were ordered by Him. It was a set-up. Notice that the king didn't say, "Hey Haman, what do you think I ought to do for Mordecai, since he spared my life?" No, neither Mordecai nor Haman are mentioned. Notice the fateful words – "What shall be done for *the man* whom the king delights to honor?" – mentioned five times in 6:6, 6:7, 6:9 (2X), and 6:11. "Haman did not even have a chance to tell the king why he was there."[166]

---

[166] See Breneman, page 345.

The haughty Haman "quickly begins to list every glory he can imagine for himself."[167] Verse 6 says, "Now Haman thought in his heart, 'Whom would the king delight to honor more than me?'" Expecting a promotion for himself, Haman says, "For the man whom the king delights to honor, let a royal robe be brought which the king has worn, and a horse on which the king has ridden, which has a royal crest placed on its head. Then let this robe and horse be delivered to the hand of one of the king's most noble princes, that he may array the man whom the king delights to honor. Then parade him on horseback through the city square, and proclaim before him: 'Thus shall it be done to the man whom the king delights to honor!'" Baldwin correctly observes, "Haman inadvertently promotes Mordecai."[168] Jobes adds, "Believing the honors would go to himself, Haman could not ask for a promotion because he was already second only to the king in his authority over the empire."[169] With a "royal robe," royal horse, and "royal crest," Haman wanted to be "honored like a king, by the king."[170] Interestingly, the Hebrew word here for "royal" (twice) is derived from the Hebrew noun for "king" or "reign." This "royalty" represented the king's "kingdom and reign." It appears that even though the honor was coming from the king, Haman wanted to be king (at least for a day)! He exalted himself so now he will be humbled.

In verse 10, Haman hears these devastating words from the king: "Hurry, take the robe and the horse, as you have suggested, and do so for Mordecai the Jew who sits within the king's gate!" What was "suggested" by Zeresh (5:14), was to be "suggested" by Haman (6:4), is now "suggested" by Haman to the king (6:10). The "suggestion" that completely humiliates Haman has been accepted. And

---

[167] See Swindoll, page 117.
[168] See Baldwin, title to chapter 6, page 88.
[169] See Jobes, page 153.
[170] See Laniak, page 242.

"the king identifies Mordecai in terms of what Haman hates most: '*The Jew*, who sits at the king's gate.'"[171] I'm sure that Haman's face turned pale. When he was done, "his head was covered" (6:12). The words – "Leave nothing undone of all that you have spoken" – were surely motivated by the Lord and must have been salt in Haman's wounds! What a bitter pill Haman had to swallow!

I would have loved to be in the locker room while Haman was putting the robe on Mordecai. What tension! What kind of expression must have been on Haman's face as he went to get that royal horse that had the royal crest on its head. To then help Mordecai get up on the horse was hard, but it must have been nerve-racking to shout the praises of Mordecai through the open square. This is total humiliation! Every word out of his mouth was filled with shame and disgrace!

Esther 6:11 is "arguably the most ironically comic scene in the entire Bible."[172] "So Haman took the robe and the horse, arrayed Mordecai and led him on horseback  through the city square, and proclaimed before him, 'Thus shall it be done to the man whom the king delights to honor!'" "The words Haman had to proclaim must have been gravel in his mouth. In the eyes of the crowd, he was already finished."[173] I noticed in 6:9 and 6:11 that Mordecai was paraded "through the city square." This is exactly where "Hathach" found Mordecai in sackcloth and ashes after Haman's decree was issued (4:6). The Lord had given him "beauty for ashes, the oil of joy for mourning, and the garment of praise for the spirit of heaviness."[174]

---

[171] See Laniak, page 239.
[172] See Jobes, page 152.
[173] See Baldwin, page 90.
[174] See Isaiah 61:3.

Before I taught the course on the Book of Esther, I watched F. Murray Abraham's movie, *Esther*. While it might be considered a B-rated movie, it is the most biblically accurate of all the available Esther films. In the movie, when Haman was taking Mordecai through the city, it shows them going past Haman's house with the 75-foot gallows in the background. I thought this was certainly possible. His house was near the palace and a structure of that height could easily have been seen by both of them. I got an eerie feeling for Haman right at that moment.

Swindoll makes this important comment about Mordecai's humble character and integrity based on Esther 6:12: "Mordecai returned to the king's gate because that's where he's been all the time. His role has not gone to his head. Are you still comfortable at the king's gate or must you now live at the palace?"[175] At the end of Esther Chapter 2, the king makes a serious oversight and fails to even acknowledge Mordecai's saving deed. He never complains. He never visits the palace office to see why he was overlooked. He never tells Esther to remind the king again about what happened even though "Esther informed the king in Mordecai's name" (2:22). That's the beauty of his life – he just kept on living a godly life as a God-fearing Jew. He wasn't concerned about position and power in King Ahasuerus's empire. If God didn't allow him to be recognized, he remained content where he was. This surely requires great strength of character. And here in verse 12, it reads, "Afterward Mordecai went back to the king's gate." Even after he is honored, he is still content in his current position "at the king's gate." It is an understatement to say that Mordecai has a humble spirit. David wrote in Psalm 37:11, "The meek shall inherit the earth, and shall delight themselves in the abundance of peace."[176] That's

---

[175] See Swindoll, pages 118-119.
[176] See also Matthew 5:5.

what I see in Mordecai and those who are "clothed with humility" – they have an "abundance of peace." They don't need a position or title to be used by God. Psalm 75:6 says, "No one from the east or the west or from the south can exalt a man. But it is God who judges: He brings one down, he exalts another." Promotion comes from God.

For those of us who are Christians, we should heed Paul's words to the Philippians: "I have learned to be content whatever the circumstances. I know what it is to be in need, and I know what it is to have plenty. I have learned the secret of being content in any and every situation, whether well fed or hungry, whether living in plenty or in want." The reason this was true was because "I can do all things through Christ who strengthens me."[177] Somehow, Mordecai had "learned the secret of being content." In today's covetous and discontented culture, this is not easy, but it is something we all desperately need.

Haman, on the other hand, "hurried to his house, mourning and with his head covered" (v12). Amazingly, just a few days earlier, the Jews were in "great mourning" along with "weeping and wailing" (4:3). The tables have begun to turn and Haman has begun to fall. Mary, the mother of Jesus, sang a song that included the lines: "He has shown strength with His arm; He has scattered the proud in the imagination of their hearts. He has put down the mighty from their thrones, and exalted the lowly. He has filled the hungry with good things, and the rich He has sent away empty." This is the contrast between Haman and Mordecai in this chapter. Everything in this song describes Haman's deep humiliation. He was "sent away empty." Everything that Haman wanted for himself is going to Mordecai. Haman's pride and Mordecai's humility are highlighted in these verses.

---

[177] See Philippians 4:11-13.

A gloomy and ominous cloud comes over Haman's life. "When Haman told his wife Zeresh and all his friends everything that had happened to him, his wise men and his wife Zeresh said to him, 'If Mordecai, before whom you have begun to fall, is of Jewish descent, you will not prevail against him but will surely fall before him'" (v13). Notice the word, "fall," mentioned twice. Laniak makes this important point: "Haman is not simply "falling;" he is falling *before Mordecai*."[178] "Pride goes before destruction, and a haughty spirit before a fall."

To hear your own wife and best friends remind you that Mordecai was "of Jewish descent" only added salt to Haman's wounds. Mordecai the Jew was going up; Haman the Agagite was going down.

Haman is fully in God's hands. He has lost all control. He cannot stop what is about to happen to him. This chapter closes with "while they were still talking with him, the king's eunuchs came, and hastened to bring Haman to the banquet which Esther had prepared" (v14). Haman has no time whatsoever to process what is happening in his life. He is no longer happy and boasting; he is now sad and mourning. "Zeresh and his wise men" were not even done talking to him when he is whisked away. Esther, however, was already waiting because she had "the banquet prepared" for the king and Haman.

In this 6th Chapter, Mordecai is honored. In the 7th Chapter, Haman is hanged. At Esther's second banquet, Haman is hanged on the very gallows he built for Mordecai. Let us now look at how Esther's secret exposes Haman's plot and leads to his death.

---

[178] Laniak, italics his, page 240.

7

Esther's Second Banquet & Haman's Hanging

*"Now Harbonah, one of the eunuchs, said to the
king, 'Look! The gallows, fifty cubits high,
which Haman made for Mordecai, who spoke
good on the king's behalf, is standing at the
house of Haman.' Then the king said, 'Hang
him on it!'" (Esther 7:9)*

One of the most sensational and suspenseful
things I ever witnessed on video was the
hanging of Iraqi dictator, Saddam Hussein,
on Saturday, December 30, 2006. The
grainy and shaky video made the scene
all the more real and eerie. This man,
who once ordered the murder and
gassing of thousands of people, was led
up a simple flight of stairs to the top of a platform. Two men
– dressed with black masks – met him. One of the men
placed a black handkerchief around his neck. The other man

placed a thick hangman's noose over his head and over the handkerchief. It's difficult to discern who is speaking, but several voices can be heard, including Saddam's, as the final moments of his life are captured on video. "God is great!" "Mohammed is God's prophet!" "Brothers!" Some people were taunting him. Others mocked.

Finally, with no advanced warning, the floor below Saddam Hussein is quickly released. He falls. Immediate pandemonium erupts. The camera moves away from seeing Saddam actually hanging to the stairs and then to a black screen. All the while, people are yelling many words in the Iraqi language. The last scene on the video shows a dead Saddam with a noose around his head. Most videos of the hanging are about two minutes and thirty seconds long. Just like that, the "butcher of Baghdad" was dead. The man who brutally suppressed all internal opposition and led his country into two devastating wars was gone.

Nearly 2,500 years earlier, we read these ominous words in Esther 7:10: "They hanged Haman on the gallows." Just like that, the man who had decreed the extermination of all the Jews in the 127 provinces of the vast Persian Empire was dead. His vain, haughty, boisterous personality was removed from the world scene and the halls of government power. Haman, "the enemy of the Jews," was hanging on the gallows in front of his own house. Ray Stedman cleverly calls Esther Chapter 7, "Haman's Last Supper."[179] Let's look carefully at this chapter that reveals his terrible demise.

Just like the first banquet, one in which Esther prepared the banquet before anyone was invited, so it was with the second banquet. Her two guests came "to the banquet which Esther had prepared" (6:14). While Haman was preparing the gallows, Esther was preparing the

---

[179] See the chapter title of his devotional study on Esther 7, page 93.

banquet. What Haman was preparing for Mordecai, Esther was preparing for Haman.

The chapter begins with these simple words: "So the king and Haman went to dine with Queen Esther." The first banquet was "the banquet of wine" (5:6); the second banquet was also "the banquet of wine" (7:2, 7:7, 7:8). Both men loved to drink and Esther was serving what they delighted in. We know that the king was very fond of wine: "They served royal wine in abundance, according to the generosity of the king," "the heart of the king was merry with wine," and "the king and Haman sat down to drink."[180] Esther had a way with words and a way with drinks. She knew what Haman and the king liked.

Now, for the third and final time, the king asks Esther in verse 2, "What is your petition, Queen Esther? It shall be granted you. And what is your request, up to half the kingdom? It shall be done!" He guarantees that she will receive whatever she asks – "It shall be granted you. It shall be done!" One commentator observes: "There is great irony in Xerxes' request. He assumed that she would ask for material possessions when in reality she was interested in what really matters: human lives. Xerxes, of course, did not know this."[181]

Finally, the moment of truth has arrived. Finally, Esther answers the king's questions. Finally, Esther reveals her Jewish identity and her concern for the Jewish people. The king has been married to a Jew all along! What a shock!

It's interesting that "both Esther and Haman plead for their lives in this chapter."[182] What does Esther say? "By framing her response using the king's rhetoric, Esther is saying that her life and the life of her people are one and the same. Her destiny is one with her people."[183] Her

---

[180] See Esther 1:7, 1:10, and 3:15.
[181] See Breneman, page 347.
[182] See Jobes, page 166.
[183] See Jobes, page 164.

completely unexpected petition is "let my life be given me." Her life is being threatened. Basically, someone wants to kill her! Who would dare do this?

Not only that, her request identifies others who are in danger: Let "my people" be given me. Then she immediately uses the very words taken from Haman's decree in Esther 3:13 – "to be destroyed, to be killed, and to be annihilated." The astonishing truth is that the threat to kill the queen was signed and sealed "in the name of King Ahasuerus" and "sealed with the king's signet ring" (3:12). Of course, Esther doesn't word it that way. "For we have been sold" is probably a reference to the "ten thousand talents of silver" (3:9) that Haman offered for this slaughter. Mordecai had highlighted to Esther "the sum of money that Haman had promised to pay into the king's treasuries to destroy the Jews" (4:7). The words, "My people and I," show how closely bound Esther is with "these people." She still hasn't used the word, "Jew(s)," nor has she mentioned "Haman" by name.

With characteristic diplomacy and sensitivity, Esther speaks to the king so as not to offend, even though she has already disclosed some sensational news. "Had we been sold as male and female slaves, I would have held my tongue." In other words, "If we were being sold into slavery, I would not have bothered you with such trivial matters." This statement only serves to heighten the severity of the death sentence on her and the Jews. What Esther is bringing up is deadly serious. Laniak says correctly, "This disclaimer effectively underscores the gravity of her request. It is also a subtle way of recalling for the king the monetary transaction that took place at their place."[184]

She now mentions someone as "the enemy" when she says: "Although the enemy could never compensate for the king's loss." Esther is telling him that if she and her

---

[184] See Laniak, page 243.

people were sold into slavery, the loss that the king would experience in terms of productivity and prosperity could never be offset or paid back (by Haman's ten thousand talents). Esther is saying, "The king will lose a lot if we go into slavery, but just think of the loss if we are killed!" The margin of the NIV reads, "The compensation our adversary offers cannot be compared with the loss the king would suffer." There's not enough money anywhere to compensate for the loss of the Jews whether by slavery or by death.

Obviously upset, the king asks Queen Esther: "Who is he, and where is he, who would dare presume in his heart to do such a thing?" That person happens to be sitting right next to him! It's his own prime minister! The person who holds the "signet ring" of absolute authority is the very one seeking to destroy the queen and her people! "The king's agitated questions in verse 5 reveal his readiness to protect his queen. Someone close to the king was plotting the destruction of his queen!"[185]

I don't think it is a coincidence that her role as queen is highlighted – "Queen Esther" (v1), "Queen Esther" (v2), "Queen Esther" (v3), "Queen Esther" (v5), and "Queen Esther" (v7). "The enemy" is not just messing around with any woman; he's attacking the queen of the Persian Empire and the wife of King Ahasuerus! This guy is in big trouble!

Without a moment's hesitation, Esther identified the person as "the adversary and enemy is this wicked Haman!" The Hebrew word for "adversary" is the same one used in 7:4 and translated "the enemy." "Tsar" in Hebrew means a foe or opponent who causes trouble. It is translated as "trouble," "distress," and "affliction" in many Old Testament books. It is used in 108 verses of the Old Testament to describe "the enemies" of God's people. The Hebrew word for "enemy" is 'oyeb which means someone who hates. It is used only here in Esther and Chapters 8 and

[185] See Laniak, page 244.

9. It is translated as the "enemies" of the Jews (8:13, 9:1, 9:5, 9:16, and 9:22). She also described him as "wicked" or "vile." It is the main Hebrew word for "evil."

Now that he has been exposed, "Haman was terrified before the king and queen." In one minute, the man who held the reins of power over a great empire is "pale with fright."[186] "*Her* enemy is now *his* enemy and thus *the enemy*."[187]

The king, a man known for his hot temper,[188] flew into a "rage" and had to leave Haman's immediate presence. "Why was the king so angry? Certainly he was angry because he had been tricked into making the decree that meant the death of his own beloved queen, Esther."[189] This chapter, which started with Esther pleading for her life, now had Haman pleading for his. The reason he did this was because "he saw that evil was determined against him by the king" (v7). The Hebrew word here for "evil" is the same one used by Esther to describe the "*wicked* Haman." The NIV says that Haman realized "that the king had already decided his fate" and the NLT reads that "the king intended to kill him."

The king "went into the palace garden" (v7) for a few minutes to cool off, but he "returned from the palace garden to the place of the banquet of wine" (v8). Haman was pleading for his life by falling all over "Esther" and "the couch." The king interpreted this action as Haman's attempt to "molest" or "assault" the queen "before my very eyes" or "with me still in the house." This only served to further enrage the king. "As soon as the word left the king's mouth,

---

[186] See the NLT translation.

[187] See Laniak, page 244.

[188] Interestingly, the Hebrew word here for "wrath" or "rage" is only used in the Book of Esther to describe the king or Haman. See Esther 1:12, 2:1, 3:5, 5:9, 7:7, and 7:10.

[189] See Breneman, page 349.

they covered Haman's face."[190] Covering his face like this "signaled his doom."[191] "Haman had fallen" in verse 8 are the perfect words to describe what happened to this proud and haughty man. "Pride goes before destruction, and a haughty spirit before a fall" says the famous proverb.[192] In the previous chapter,  Zeresh had predicted that her husband "had begun to fall" and "you will surely fall" (6:14).

Jobes explains that "even in the presence of others, a man was not to approach a woman of the king's harem within seven steps."[193] Laniak says, "The king returns to find what he identifies as attempted rape. The term 'molest' refers to either sexual or military assault and subjugation. A sexual advance on the wife or concubine of an ancient king was tantamount to a run on the throne."[194] Even in pleading for his life, Haman can do nothing right. His death is now assured.

In another moment of divine providence and perfect timing, "Harbonah," one of the "seven eunuchs who served in the presence of King Ahasuerus" (1:10), informs the king: "Look! The gallows, fifty cubits high, which Haman made for Mordecai, who spoke good on the king's behalf, is standing at the house of Haman." Apparently, knowledge of the incredible height of "the gallows" had spread to even the king's palace. Originally, only Zeresh and Haman's friends knew the height, but now Harbonah knows the dimensions.

---

[190] The "covering of the face" reminds me of how they covered the faces of the conspirators who were hanged for plotting the assassination of President Abraham Lincoln. The first to be hung were David Herold, Lewis Powell, George Atzerodt and Mary Surratt.
[191] See the NLT translation of Esther 7:8.
[192] See Proverbs 16:18.
[193] See Jobes, page 165.
[194] See Laniak, page 245.

He also knew that "Haman made the gallows for Mordecai." And Mordecai was the person who just the day before was honored by the king for sparing his life. He was the one "who spoke good on the king's behalf." *The king now realizes that Haman was planning to kill both his wife and the person who saved his life!* Aroused now to extreme anger, it only makes sense that the king said, "Hang him on it!" Haman is hung on "the gallows that he had prepared for Mordecai" (v10).

Is not Haman's life a sad example of a biblical truth – *the evil you wish upon others will come upon you*? If you dig a pit, you will fall into it. If you judge others, you will be judged. If you sow evil, you will reap it.

There is a song that the Jews sing even today during the Feast of Purim. One line from this song is "He (Haman) who sought to trap was trapped instead; he who planned destruction was himself destroyed."[195] Consider these Old Testament verses:

- Proverbs 26:27 – "Whoever digs a pit will fall into it, and he who rolls a stone will have it roll back on him."
- Psalm 7:15-16 – "They dig a deep pit to trap others, then fall into it themselves. The trouble they make for others backfires on them. The violence they plan falls on their own heads."
- Psalm 9:15 – "The nations have fallen into the pit they dug for others. Their own feet have been caught in the trap they set."
- Psalm 57:6 – "They have dug a deep pit in my path, but they themselves have fallen into it."
- Ecclesiastes 10:8 – "He who digs a pit will fall into it."

---

[195] See *Megillat Esther* by Robert Gordis, New York, page 93, quoted by Jobes, page 218.

I don't want to miss this tragic point: The gallows were "standing at the house of Haman." Haman was so filled with rage and indignation against "Mordecai that Jew" that he wanted to see him hanging right in front of his house. And it was Haman's own wife, "Zeresh," and "all his friends" who recommended the building of the gallows. I think that Zeresh may be one of the most tragic figures in the entire Bible. As we will see in the 9th chapter, not only was her husband hung in front of her house, so were her ten sons! Esther 9:25 reads, "The wicked plot which Haman had devised against the Jews should return on his own head, and that he and his sons should be hanged on the gallows." What a terrible sight for a wife and mother to behold! Esther said, "Let Haman's ten sons be hanged on the gallows" (9:13). The king again granted her request: "So the king commanded this to be done; the decree was issued in Shushan, and they hanged Haman's ten sons" (9:14). This is a fate even worse than Job's.[196] What Zeresh advised Haman for Mordecai came upon her. Haman was dead; thus, Zeresh experienced the hanging deaths of all ten sons by herself!

After a tense chapter filled with crisis and drama, it ends with the calm words – "Then the king's wrath subsided."

It has been my observation that for many Christians, Haman's death represents the end of the Book of Esther. The bad guy is dead. The main antagonist has been killed. Next story.

Nothing could be further from the truth. Esther was spared by the king. Mordecai was delivered out of the hands of his enemy. But what about all the Jews in the Persian

---

[196] See Job 1:18-19. He lost "seven sons and three daughters" (1:2), all of his children, when a "great wind" struck the oldest son's house and caused the roof and walls to collapse on all of them.

Empire? Breneman makes the key point: "The story is not over. The narrative has shown the rise and fall of Haman, but the edict of annihilation is still intact. More is at stake here than just Mordecai's life; also at stake are the lives of all the Jews in the Persian Empire."[197] Haman is dead, but his decree is still alive. The next two chapters (8-9) tell us the story of how the decree to annihilate the Jews is overcome. The plot only thickens. Now, not just Esther and Mordecai are in danger, the entire Jewish race is marked out for extermination. The ultimate Jewish holocaust looms just around the corner.

Haman's decree "to destroy, to kill, and to annihilate" all the Jews was signed "in the name of King Ahasuerus" and sealed with his "signet ring." Chapter 3 calls it "the king's command" (see also 4:3 and 9:1). Mordecai's decree for the Jews "to destroy, to kill, and to annihilate" all their enemies was signed "in the name of King Ahasuerus" and sealed with his "signet ring." Chapter 8 calls it "the king's command" (8:14, 8:17). Both decrees could not be revoked. Both decrees could not be altered.[198] The king stated plainly that "whatever is written in the king's name and sealed with the king's signet ring no one can revoke" (8:10). Haman's decree versus Mordecai's decree; the Amalekite versus the Jew; the king's command versus the king's command; this heavyweight battle will take place on "one day,"[199] "the thirteenth day, in the twelfth month, the month of Adar." Chapter 9 gives us the details of this battle.

---

[197] See Breneman, page 350.

[198] Recall here how Daniel was thrown into the lions' den when a decree signed by King Darius that "cannot be changed" and "which does not alter." See Daniel 6:8, 6:12, 6:15, and 6:17.

[199] Remember that Mordecai's decree was valid for only "one day" as Esther 8:12 states plainly. The Jews could only fight on the thirteenth of Adar. In fact, Esther had to ask permission of the king for the Jews to fight the next day, the fourteenth (9:13-15).

No, the fight is not over with Haman's death. His decree must also be defeated by all the Jewish people themselves. Let us now go to the exciting 8th chapter, as Mordecai gets promoted to prime minister over all of the Persian Empire and issues a decree for the Jews to defend themselves against Haman's decree. The king will also give "the house of Haman" or "the estate of Haman" to Queen Esther who then gives it to Mordecai. The man whom Haman despised and hated now has complete control of "his great riches" (5:11).

8

Esther's Intervention & Mordecai's Decree

*"Then King Ahasuerus said to Queen Esther
and Mordecai the Jew, 'Indeed, I have given
Esther the house of Haman, and they have
hanged him on the gallows because he tried to
lay his hand on the Jews. You yourselves write
a decree concerning the Jews, as you please, in
the king's name, and seal it with the king's
signet ring; for whatever is written in the king's
name and sealed with the king's signet ring no
one can revoke.'" (Esther 8:7-8)*

"**H**aman may be dead, but the edict is still very much alive. It has been written; it will be done!"[200] "Esther had saved the Jews from Haman, but not from his handiwork: the death document."[201] Haman is dead; his decree is alive. What will

---

[200] See Swindoll, page 143.
[201] See Breneman, page 352.

Esther do now? How will she or Mordecai revoke the irrevocable?

Verse 1 starts, "On that day King Ahasuerus gave Queen Esther the house of Haman, the enemy of the Jews. And Mordecai came before the king, for Esther had told how he was related to her." "On that day" is translated "on that same day" or "by the end of the day" in other translations. The verse just before this one indicates that it was the day "they hanged Haman on the gallows" (7:10). The king, not Queen Esther, took some serious action. The king gave the queen "everything that belonged to Haman"[202] – "the house," "the property," or "the entire estate" of Haman. In Esther 8:7, King Ahasuerus says, "Indeed, I have given Esther the house of Haman." All of the "great riches" of Haman now belonged to Queen Esther. There is a proverb that says, "The wealth of the sinner is stored up for the righteous."[203] I don't know for sure, but this may have been one of the key reasons why Esther had to eliminate Haman's "ten sons" (9:7-14, 9:25). Surely, these sons would have wanted their father's great wealth.

Haman is again identified as "the enemy of the Jews" (3:10, 9:10, 9:24). What an amazing turnaround in just 24 hours! At the beginning of the day, Haman is on his way to see the king to hang Mordecai, and before the day is over, Haman is dead and all of his possessions belong to Queen Esther who gives them to Mordecai! Surely, God's hands were in this transfer of wealth and power from the enemy.

For the first time in the story, Esther tells King Ahasuerus that Mordecai is actually his older cousin and the "father" who raised her. Now that that secret is out, it gives Mordecai immediate access into the king's presence – "And Mordecai came before the king." The full transfer of power will move quickly from here.

---

[202] See the ERV Translation.
[203] See Proverbs 13:22.

We are not told exactly how, but before Haman was whisked away to be hanged, the king made sure that he got back that all-important "signet ring." The king "had taken the ring from Haman" (8:2) and then put it on his hand. Verse 2 says, "So the king took off his signet ring and gave it to Mordecai." With that simple act, a tremendous transfer of authority and responsibility are now on Mordecai's shoulders. God's truth prevails – the humble are exalted. "Mordecai was not a prophet or a miracle worker, nor did he rule as king in Jerusalem. He wore the signet ring of a Persian king, not the ephod of the high priest."[204] There is now a concentration of government power on Mordecai – he takes Haman's position; he assumes control over Haman's "estate" (v2); he issues an empire-wide decree and "commands" all Jews, satraps, governors, and princes (v9); and he is crowned and robed in royalty (v15). Haman must be turning over in his grave!

Verse 2 closes with the words, "And Esther appointed Mordecai over the house of Haman." Laniak notes, "The Hebrew word for 'appointed' is the one used to refer to the king's promotion of Haman in 3:1. How things have changed since the days when the young Jewess did all that Mordecai commanded. He is now the steward of her estate."[205] He does not become the owner but rather the manager of what belongs to Esther. Haman's devastating fall is countered by Mordecai's meteoric rise. "Whoever exalts himself will be humbled, and he who humbles himself will be exalted."[206]

A second time she approaches unsummoned, but this time "with tears" and again "the king held out the golden scepter" (8:4).[207] The desperate situation is easily observed

---

[204] See Jobes, page 213.
[205] See Laniak, page 248.
[206] See Matthew 23:12; Luke 14:11, 18:14.
[207] Breneman observes, "This time the scepter was not raised to save Esther's life but rather to show that she is more than welcome in the

because Esther "fell down at his feet" and "implored him with tears" (8:3). In verse 6, we read, "How can I endure" or "how can I bear to see" are written twice indicating truly how unbearable it was for Esther.

She wanted "to counteract the evil of Haman the Agagite, and the scheme which he had devised against the Jews." Remember, Esther has to be careful here, because the decree was "written in the name of King Ahasuerus," "signed with the king's signet ring," and known as "the king's command." This was a delicate matter. Her words are again filled with grace and humility – "If it pleases the king, and if I have found favor in his sight and the thing seems right to the king and I am pleasing in his eyes." Esther wisely lays the blame at the feet of "Haman the Agagite" and not the king. Esther tells the king "to revoke the letters *devised by Haman*, the son of Hammedatha the Agagite, which *he wrote* to annihilate the Jews who are in all the king's provinces" (8:5, italics mine). She eliminates any type of accusation against the king. "The letters" that Esther refers to are "the letters sent by couriers into all the king's provinces, to destroy, to kill and to annihilate all the Jews" (3:13). The letters contained "the evil...against the Jews" (v3), "to annihilate the Jews" (v5), "the evil to my people," and "the destruction of my countrymen" (v6). In other words, Haman himself, not the king, had planned the ultimate holocaust.

Esther wants "to revoke" (v4) what "no one can revoke" (v8).[208] She is now relying on the king to tell her how "to counteract" (v3) what Haman has done. His answer is very simple: *Issue another decree.* This becomes the main subject of verses 8-14 of this chapter. But isn't it tragic that "the king himself is a prisoner of the law he created? Even

king's presence. Thus the king's act of extending the scepter was simply an encouragement to Esther to rise and speak." (Which Esther does at the end of verse 4). See Breneman, page 352.
[208] Remember Daniel 6:8 and 6:12.

though he changes his mind, he cannot change what he signed."[209] As Pilate once said, "What I have written, I have written."[210] Once a powerful dictator or ruler issues a decree, there is no going back. These rulers did not govern under a republic or democracy with its checks and balances.

I don't want to miss an important word that resurfaces again here. We last saw it in Chapter 3. It is the word, "Agagite." Verses 3 and 5 say respectively, "The evil of Haman *the Agagite*" and "the letters devised by Haman *the Agagite*." The author is saying let's not forget what this is about. This is about the ancient hostility between God and the Amalekites. This is not some personal vengeance on Esther's part. This is not about Mordecai getting his revenge on Haman. No, this is about God's war against the Amalekites that began in one of the earliest books of the Bible – Exodus.

Verse 7 says, "Then King Ahasuerus said to Queen Esther and Mordecai the Jew, 'Indeed, I have given Esther the house of Haman, and they have hanged him on the gallows because he tried to lay his hand on the Jews.'" This verse tells us why Haman was hanged – "because he tried to lay his hand on the Jews." Of course, the two main ones were "Queen Esther and Mordecai the Jew." As we wrote somewhere else in this book, one of the Jews saved his life and the other one was his wife! Haman was inadvertently coming against the two most important people in the king's life. No wonder Haman was hanged.

"You yourselves write a decree concerning the Jews, as you please, in the king's name, and seal it with the king's signet ring; for whatever is written in the king's name and sealed with the king's signet ring no one can revoke." The king tells both Queen Esther and Mordecai to write another irrevocable decree. This is the only way to counter what

---

[209] See Stedman, pages 108-109.
[210] See John 19:22.

Haman did in Chapter 3. And these two decrees will come head to head in a battle to the death in the next chapter, Chapter 9. "You yourselves" indicate that the king gave permission to both of them to compose the decree, and "write a decree" is an imperative verb in Hebrew, so the king was commanding them to write it. The king gives Queen Esther and Mordecai the Jew a blank check to issue a decree "as you please." The king had earlier given a similar command to Haman – "Do with them as seems good to you" (3:11).

For emphasis, the king uses "the king's name" and "the king's signet ring." Again, once something is "sealed," "no one can revoke" it. That's why the king never told Esther to just tear up the old decree or write another decree revoking Haman's decree. Again, Persian decrees or laws signed by the king could not be revoked or annulled. Again, "The only solution to their dilemma is to write another decree to counteract the first with equal force."[211]

Verse 9 is the longest verse in the Bible. In the King James Version, it has ninety words. The "king's scribes were called in at that time, in the third month, which is the month of Sivan, on the twenty-third day." We have to recall the date of Haman's decree in Esther 3:12 to understand the significance of this new date. Haman's decree was written "on the thirteenth day of the first month" or March 13th. Mordecai's decree was written on "the twenty-third day of the third month" or May 23rd. "Sivan," which is used only here in the entire Bible, is the month of May. So Mordecai's decree was written exactly seventy days after Haman's. Some commentators try to make a symbolic connection with the "seventy years of exile," but this is not necessary, and besides, the Bible makes no mention here of the exile or even attaching any significance to these "seventy days." The author was merely telling us the date that Mordecai's decree

---

[211] See Jobes, page 177.

was written. That's all we need to know, so there's no need to spiritualize the text or read something more into the date.

What we do know is that the scribes "wrote down" everything "written by Mordecai." So apparently, the principal author of the decree was Mordecai. In fact, after Esther 8:7, Esther is not mentioned again until Esther 9:12. She may have advised him on the decree, but Mordecai put together the final wording.

The remaining language of the verse gives us the comprehensive scope of who was to receive the decree. No one in the Persian Empire is left out – "To the Jews, the satraps, the governors, and the princes of the provinces from India to Ethiopia, one hundred and twenty-seven provinces in all, to every province in its own script, to every people in their own language, and to the Jews in their own script and language." The bottom-line is this: It was written to everybody in every province in every language. It is important to observe, that unlike the wording of Haman's decree, this decree was first "to the Jews" and "to the Jews in their own script and language." Perhaps they were some of the first ones to receive the decree. Certainly, this would be possible for the Jews living in Shushan (see the end of verse 14). The decree went from India to Ethiopia. The Hebrew word here for "Ethiopia," is "Kuwsh" or "Cush."[212] The only other place in Esther where this Hebrew word is found is in the opening verse of the book – "King Ahasuerus reigned over 127 provinces, from India to *Ethiopia*."

Esther 8:10, "And he wrote in the name of King Ahasuerus, sealed it with the king's signet ring, and sent letters by couriers on horseback, riding on royal horses bred from swift steeds." If Mordecai lived in today's world of modern communications and transportation, he surely would

---

[212] "Kuwsh" is always translated "Ethiopia" instead of "Cush" except in Genesis 10:6-8 and 1 Chronicles 1:8-10 when describing Ham's son who became Nimrod's father. See also Isaiah 11:11. (NKJV Translation).

have used overnight, express service. Baldwin writes, "Mordecai evidently went to extreme lengths to ensure the express delivery of his new edict."[213] Verse 14 notes, "The couriers who rode on royal horses went out, hastened and pressed on by the king's command." The NCV says, "The messengers hurried out, riding on the royal horses, because the king commanded those messengers to hurry." This was an urgent word. The NLT says that the couriers "rode fast horses especially bred for the king's service" or they "rode the king's finest and fastest horses."

In order to counter Haman's decree that was also written "in the name of King Ahasuerus" and "sealed with the king's signet ring," Mordecai had to do the same. The same word for "couriers" used by Haman in 3:13 and 3:15 are used here in 8:10 and 8:14.

I think it is important to bring up at this point the roll of the dice in 3:7. The edict ("these letters," 8:11) has to go by royal horses to all 127 provinces. There is now plenty of time to get the word out and for the Jews to arm themselves. If the sorcerers rigged the rolling of the dice to land within a few weeks of the decree's fateful date, then the Jews would have been destroyed. The hand of God overruled the affairs of men. The Lord, though invisible in the story, made sure that the dice landed on the thirteenth day of Adar, which was still about nine months away. The providence of God prevails.

Verse 11 tells us that it was by Mordecai's decree that the king (not Mordecai) allowed the Jews to defend themselves – "the king permitted the Jews." This was all an act of self-defense. The king was even giving them permission to "plunder their possessions." Haman's decree allowed for this as well (3:13), but the Jews never did that – "but they did not lay a hand on the plunder" (9:10), "but they did not lay a hand on the plunder" (9:15), and "but they did

---

[213] See Baldwin, page 96.

not lay a hand on the plunder" (9:16). Jobes writes, "Mordecai's decree included the permission to plunder because he was reversing the exact terms that Haman's decree had previously established."[214] The Jews will be able to do to others what their enemies intended to do to them.

I want to point out something here that is very important for the interpretation of Bible verses. What do you do with biblical language that seems morally wrong here in verse 11? Let's not shrink back from the wording here: The king is giving the Jews permission to "destroy, kill and annihilate all the forces of any people or province that would assault them, *both little children and women.*" What are we to do with something that makes the Jews look barbaric?

Notice something we should never do – try to change the language of the biblical text to get it to say something it is not saying. That's what some of the modern translations like the NIV and NLT do. The Hebrew text definitely indicates that the Jews can kill the "women and children" of their attackers, but the NIV rewords it to make it more palatable: "The king's edict granted the Jews in every city the right to assemble and protect themselves; to destroy, kill and annihilate any armed force of any nationality or province that might attack them and their women and children; and to plunder the property of their enemies." This translation makes it sound like the Jews should attack anyone who attacks "*their* women and children." This is not what the Hebrew text is saying. Listen also to the NLT: "The king's decree gave the Jews in every city authority to unite to defend their lives. They were allowed to kill, slaughter, and annihilate anyone of any nationality or province who might attack them or their children and wives, and to take the property of their enemies." Again, this translation makes it appear that the Jews can retaliate on anyone attacking the *Jewish* "women and children." This sounds very righteous

---

[214] See Jobes, page 196.

and heroic. Of course, that's what men should do to protect their families from brutal attackers, but that's not the wording of the original language. It clearly reads like the NKJV, "...to destroy, kill and annihilate...all forces that assault them, both little children and women." I'm not trying to be barbaric myself; I'm trying to stay with the text. Jobes makes some key observations on this issue: "Even though the decree gave the Jews permission to kill the women and children of their enemies, it was not necessarily carried out. In fact, when the killing in Susa is reported, the body count refers only to 'men' (9:6, 9:12). However, when the final count of 75,000 dead is given, the reference is more generally to the 'enemies' (9:16)." "The decree permitted the Jews only to defend themselves 'against attackers,' making it a matter of self-defense. If the Jews did attack their enemies indiscriminately, their actions exceeded the permission of the decree."[215] I agree with these conclusions.

Let us remind ourselves that this was not a decree directly from God, but from "the king." It was against "any people that would assault them," so it was an act of self-defense, and as Jobes pointed out, it appears that most of the people killed were *men* who attacked the Jews. Again, the point I'm making here is let's not twist the biblical text to get it to say what we want it to say. The Bible should speak to us; we should not speak to the Bible. This always gets us into dangerous territory. This is one of the reasons why many false doctrines are passed on from generation to generation. Let us heed Peter's warning regarding the Word of God: "Some things are hard to understand, which untaught and unstable people twist to their own destruction, as they do also the rest of the Scriptures."[216] Don't twist the Word.

---

[215] Ibid, page 182.
[216] See 2 Peter 3:16.

Someone once asked me, who were "all the forces of any people or province?" In other words, who exactly were the enemies of the Jews besides Haman and maybe his sons? The book of Esther never tells us. In the next chapter, it calls them "those who hated them" (9:1), "all their enemies" (9:5), they "killed five hundred men" (9:12), "three hundred men" (9:15), "and seventy-five thousand of their enemies." The truth is we will never know. As we mentioned in Chapter 3, with all the anti-Semitism in this world, and the vastness of the Persian Empire, there were plenty of enemies who hated the Jews. Haman was just the main leader.

Verse 12 reads, "On one day in all the provinces of King Ahasuerus, on the thirteenth day of the twelfth month, which is the month of Adar." The lot was cast "to determine the day and the month" (3:7). Haman wrote that the annihilation of the Jews should take place "in one day" (3:13). He wanted their destruction done quickly. Now Mordecai's decree allows the Jews "one day" to defend themselves. It was on "the thirteenth day of the twelfth month, which is the month of Adar." This was February 13th. When commenting on this one day, Baldwin says, "Such killing was liable to escalate into an on-going vendetta, but by specifying the date, limits were set and the bloodshed contained."[217]

Because the Jews are only allowed to defend themselves for one day, Esther will have to ask permission from the king in 9:13 "to do again tomorrow according to today's decree." In Shushan, that allowed the Jews to kill another "three hundred men." Esther 8:12 is simply telling us that the Jews can defend themselves in all the provinces of the king on February 13th only.

Verse 13 says, "A copy of the document was to be issued as a decree in every province and published for all people, so that the Jews would be ready on that day to avenge

---

[217] See Baldwin, page 98.

themselves on their enemies." Because they did not have any electronic communication or copy machines back in Esther's day, handwritten copies of the decree had to be made. This decree or document had to be "issued" and "published" in "every province" and "for all people." Of course, at least 127 copies had to be made for the provinces, but with "every script and language," we know that many more copies in every language had to be written. Perhaps several hundred documents had to go out. All of them were copies of the original or translation of the original. Perhaps the most important place that this "decree was issued" was in the capital city of "Shushan the citadel" (8:14). When Esther requests more time in Chapter 9, apparently, "Shushan" is the only place the new "one day" decree is issued (see 9:14).

It was "on that day," the thirteenth of Adar, that they could "avenge themselves of their enemies." Again, no mention is made of exactly who they are.

The focus of the story turns with verses 15-16. "So Mordecai went out from the presence of the king in royal apparel of blue and white, with a great crown of gold and a garment of fine linen and purple; and the city of Shushan rejoiced and was glad. The Jews had light and gladness, joy and honor." "Mordecai receives the ring Haman had worn but also symbols of royalty that Haman had only dreamed of."[218] The more we want title and position, the more it seems to elude us. Somehow Mordecai was "crowned" and honored as the new "prime minister" or "second to the king" (10:3), but we are not told how or when. We will say more about Mordecai's exaltation in the next two chapters, but suffice it to say now, that Mordecai has "royal robes" of "blue and white" along with "a garment of fine linen and purple." Interestingly, the queens "Vashti" (1:11) and "Esther" (2:17) are the only ones wearing a "royal crown,"

---

[218] See Laniak, page 251.

but now Mordecai is wearing "a great crown of gold." Not just the Jews only, but also the whole "city of Shushan" begins to "rejoice" and "be glad." Here are some verses from Proverbs that apply here: "When the righteous are in authority, the people rejoice; but when a wicked man rules, the people groan" and "when it goes well with the righteous, the city rejoices; and when the wicked perish, there is jubilation."[219] With Haman gone and Mordecai in power, everyone rejoices. Corrupt governors and rulers can determine our spiritual attitude. We'll either rejoice or be depressed.

The final verse of this chapter says, "And in every province and city, wherever the king's command and decree came, the Jews had joy and gladness, a feast and a holiday. Then many of the people of the land became Jews, because fear of the Jews fell upon them." Where before (3:15-4:3) there is perplexity, bewilderment, wailing, weeping, and great mourning, now there is "rejoicing, gladness, joy, honor, feasting, and a holiday."

First of all, "Only here in the Old Testament is reference made to people of other races becoming Jews. The verb used only here means 'they Judaized themselves,' but by what process is not disclosed."[220] Laniak comments, "Gentiles will 'become Jews' in 8:17, signaling new safety and value in that identity, in contrast to the choice to keep it secret in 2:10 and 2:20."[221] How the times have changed. Before, no one was to know that Mordecai and Esther were Jews; now everyone wants to be a Jew! The tables have turned. Also, in 9:2 and 9:3, we see that "no one could withstand them, *because the fear of them fell upon all people*" and "All those doing the king's work, helped the Jews, *because the fear of Mordecai fell upon them*." This

---

[219] See Proverbs 29:2 and 11:10.
[220] See Baldwin, page 99.
[221] See Laniak, page 247.

was the fear of God among the people. The visible hand of the invisible God was at work. God promised in the Law, "This day I will begin to put the dread and fear of you upon the nations under the whole heaven, who shall hear the report of you, and shall tremble and be in anguish because of you."[222]

I have already quoted some verses from Proverbs. Here are two more that apply to Esther 8:17: "When the righteous rejoice, there is great glory; but when the wicked arise, men hide themselves" and "when the wicked arise, men hide themselves; but when they perish, the righteous increase."[223] When people like Haman are in authority, people will "hide themselves." Wicked rulers bring a dark fear among the people that causes them to hide. In many countries of the world today, people are running and hiding from powerful rulers who crush them. Many people just flee the country. Others go into exile. Proverbs 28:15-16 says, "Like a roaring lion and a charging bear is a wicked ruler over poor people. A ruler who lacks understanding is a great oppressor." When these terrible rulers "perish," righteous people "rejoice" and "increase." There is "great glory" everywhere. The people will celebrate in the streets.

Finally, the decree was seen as "the king's command" (8:17) even though it was what "Mordecai commanded" (8:9). Haman's decree was also known as the "king's command" (3:15, 4:3, 9:1). Mordecai's decree versus Haman's decree – this will be the titanic battle that is unleashed in Esther Chapter 9. Even though Haman is dead, his deadly decree is alive. Mordecai is alive, and his decree will empower the Jews to defend themselves against Haman's plot.

---

[222] See Deuteronomy 2:25.
[223] See Proverbs 28:12 and 28:28.

Let's now study the longest chapter in Esther to see how the Jews came out victorious and established a feast that is still celebrated by Jews today.

THE BOOK OF ESTHER

9

The Feast of Purim & the Triumph of the Jews

"That these days should be remembered and kept throughout every generation, every family, every province, and every city, that these days of Purim should not fail to be observed among the Jews, and that the memory of them should not perish among their descendants." (Esther 9:28)

There are dates which are forever etched in history of the United States.

June 6, 1944. On this day, commonly known as "D-Day," about 120,000 troops led by U.S. Army general, Dwight D. Eisenhower, landed at five different beaches on the coast of Normandy in northern France. There were twenty U.S. divisions, eighteen British, three Canadian, and one each from France and Poland. They came from five different cities along the southern coast of England. After crossing the English Channel, they were met by a strong force of 50,000 Germans led by General Erwin

Rommel. There were 5,000 allied casualties on the first day. However, by the end of that day, all five beaches were securely in the hands of allied forces. By the end of the month, there were 850,000 troops and 150,000 vehicles in France. Many historians consider the D-Day invasion the greatest military achievement of the 20th Century. It was part of "Operation Overlord," the allied invasion of Normandy.

December 7, 1941. President Franklin D. Roosevelt famously said it was a day that will "live in infamy." On the next day, he opened a joint session of Congress with these words: "Mr. Vice President, Mr. Speaker, Members of the Senate, and of the House of Representatives: Yesterday, December 7th, 1941 – a date which will live in infamy – the United States of America was suddenly and deliberately attacked by naval and air forces of the Empire of Japan."

Early in the morning of December 7, 1941, Japanese submarines and carrier-based planes attacked the U.S. Pacific fleet at Pearl Harbor, Hawaii. Nearby military airfields were also attacked by the Japanese planes. Eight American battleships and thirteen other naval vessels were sunk or badly damaged, almost 200 American aircraft were destroyed, and approximately 3,000 naval and military personnel were killed or wounded. The attack marked the entrance of Japan into World War II on the side of Germany and Italy, and the entrance of the United States on the Allied side.[224]

September 11, 2001. At 8:24:38 a.m. on this fateful day, the lead plotter of the 9/11 attacks, Mohammed Atta, delivered the following transmission from American Airlines Flight 11: "We have some planes. Just stay quiet,

---

[224] This paragraph was taken from the Microsoft Encarta Encyclopedia on the Pearl Harbor attack.

and you'll be okay. We are returning to the airport."[225] Before the day was over, nearly 3,000 people had died when four commercial aircraft crashed into the twin towers in New York, the Pentagon building in Washington D.C., and an open field in Somerset County, Pennsylvania. This day not only changed America forever; it changed the world forever. All you need to say is "Nine-Eleven," two numbers, and most people will know what you're talking about.

March 13th, 474 B.C. This was the day that the wicked Haman had picked (by divination) to "destroy"[226] the Jews. The decree was simple and chilling – "To destroy, to kill and to annihilate all the Jews, both young and old, little children and women, *in one day*, on the thirteenth day of the twelfth month, which is the month of Adar, and to plunder their possessions."[227] This was to be the ultimate holocaust. Every Jew in the massive Persian Empire was to be killed "*in one day*." No one can doubt that this "wicked plot" (9:25) was conceived and inspired by the devil himself. Jesus said of him, "He was a murderer from the beginning."[228]

Mordecai issued a counter-decree, however. He wrote letters whereby "the king permitted the Jews who were in every city to gather together and protect their lives – to destroy, kill, and annihilate all the forces of any people or province that would assault them, both little children and women, and to plunder their possessions, *on one day* in all

---

[225] *The 9/11 Commission Report*, Final Report of the National Commission on Terrorist Attacks Upon the United States, W. W. Norton & Company, New York, New York, page 19.

[226] Haman told the king in Esther 3:9, "Let a decree be written that they be *destroyed*."

[227] See Esther 3:13.

[228] See John 8:44.

the provinces of King Ahasuerus, on the thirteenth day of the twelfth month, which is the month of Adar."[229]

So the titanic clash was set: "Haman's decree" written "in the name of King Ahasuerus," and "sealed with the king's signet ring" is considered "the king's command" versus "Mordecai's decree" written "in the name of King Ahasuerus," and "sealed with the king's signet ring" is also considered "the king's command." Two irrevocable commands, both issued in the name of the king, both sealed by the king's ring of authority, and both could not be altered or changed, will face off in Esther, Chapter 9. "In one day," Haman wanted all the Jews dead; "on one day," Mordecai wanted all the Jews to defend themselves. March 13th was a "Friday the 13th" day for the Jews.

The first verse of Chapter 9 begins with the day in question: "Now in the twelfth month, that is, the month of Adar, on the thirteenth day, the time came for the king's command and his decree to be executed." D-Day was here. It was time to attack. The nearly year wait was over.

It is "on that day" that "the enemies of the Jews" (v1) would come out. Notice how this becomes the dominant word in Chapter 9: "The *enemies* of the Jews" (v1), "all their *enemies*" (v5), "from their *enemies*" (v16), "seventy-five thousand of their *enemies*" (v16), and "from their *enemies*" (v22). Again, Haman is cited as "the *enemy* of the Jews" (v10) and "the *enemy* of all the Jews" (v24). They are also described as "those who hated them" (v1) and "those who hated them" (v5). Interestingly, other than Haman and his ten sons, we are never told who "the enemies" were. We are only told how many of them died.

Haman and these enemies "had hoped to overpower" the Jews, but "the opposite occurred" (v2). The NIV says, "The tables were turned." Breneman is right when he says, "The sense is clearly that God had caused the tables to

---

[229] See Esther 8:11-12.

turn."[230] The hopes of their enemies were dashed because "the Jews themselves overpowered them" (v1). Now, verses 2-5 describe how the Jews overcame them.

It is easy to miss the first key element of the Jews' victory found in verse 2. Observe these simple, but powerful, words: "The Jews who were in every city *gathered together*" (8:11), "the Jews *gathered together* in their cities" (9:2), "the Jews who were in Shushan *gathered together* again" (9:15), "the Jews in the king's provinces *gathered together*" (9:16), and "the Jews who were at Shushan *assembled together*" (9:18). *When God's people are attacked, they must "gather together."* This is going to be the key to victory for the last-days' church. They gathered in "Shushan," "in every city," and "in their cities." They were not simply exiles; they were Jews. They were God's people. This is why "the Jews, instead of being the victims, became the victors on that day."[231] This is why "Esther is a story about falling and standing – the Jews' enemies fall, and the Jewish people stand."[232]

Whenever we see God's people or God's leaders under attack, we need to gather together. Call the church together. Stop the usual meetings. Gather together to pray and fast. Gather together to plan a strategy for victory. Don't just sit there and condemn someone who is under fire. Get in the fight with them. Recently, a whole army of intercessors gathered around my wife and I when the enemy attacked one of our adult children. After about two weeks of intense prayer and fasting from people all over the country, we experienced a powerful victory from the hand of the Lord! When King Jehoshaphat was under attack from "a great multitude," "Judah *gathered together* to ask help from the Lord; and from all the cities of Judah they came to seek

---

[230] See Breneman, page 358.
[231] See Baldwin, page 103.
[232] See Laniak, page 255.

the Lord."[233] When the apostle Peter was arrested, thrown into prison, and awaited execution, "Many were *gathered together* praying" and "constant prayer was offered to God for him by the church."[234]

The Jews took the initiative. They did not wait to be attacked and then defend themselves. No, they went on the offensive. They "laid hands on those who sought their harm" (v2). The author adds, "And no one could withstand them, because fear of them fell upon all people." We already saw this at the end of Chapter 8, "…because fear of the Jews fell upon them" (8:17). The next verse says, "…because the fear of Mordecai fell upon them." This definitely indicates God's hand against the enemies of the Jews. God was with them. The Jews were not barely beating their enemies. The text says that they "overpowered those who hated them" and "no one could withstand them." I like Jobes' conclusion: "The Jews are not only delivered from annihilation but are empowered."[235] I believe this is one of the reasons why only the deaths of the enemies are reported. I'm sure some Jews died, but 75,800 enemies lost their lives. This battle did not belong to the Jews; it belonged to the Lord. The visible hand of the invisible God was seen in the defeat of their enemies.

Another key reason why the Jews prevailed was because of God's favor with "all the officials of the provinces, the satraps, the governors, and all those doing the king's work" (v3). These government leaders "helped the Jews." These "satraps, governors, and the princes of the provinces from India to Ethiopia, one hundred and twenty-seven in all" had previously been commanded by Mordecai to follow his decree (8:9). Now, "the fear of Mordecai fell upon them." Mordecai was given powerful authority in the Persian kingdom. The king personally gave him his "signet

---

[233] See 2 Chronicles 20:4.
[234] See Acts 12:12 and 12:5.
[235] See Jobes, page 39.

ring" (8:2) and he "went out from the presence of the king in royal apparel of blue and white, with a great crown of gold and a garment of fine linen and purple" (8:15). It is not surprising that Esther 9:4 reads, "For Mordecai was great in the king's palace, and his fame spread throughout all the provinces; for this man Mordecai became increasingly prominent." The last chapter will speak of "the greatness of Mordecai" and that "Mordecai the Jew was second to King Ahasuerus" (10:2-3). Mordecai had what Haman always wanted. I'm reminded here of what happened to Joseph in Egypt. "You shall be over my house, and all my people shall be ruled according to your word; only in regard to the throne will I be greater than you. And Pharaoh said to Joseph, 'See, I have set you over all the land of Egypt.' Then Pharaoh took his signet ring off his hand and put it on Joseph's hand; and he clothed him in garments of fine linen and put a gold chain around his neck. And he had him ride in the second chariot which he had; and they cried out before him, 'Bow the knee!' So he set him over all the land of Egypt. Pharaoh also said to Joseph, 'I am Pharaoh, and without your consent no man may lift his hand or foot in all the land of Egypt.'"[236] Daniel, Shadrach, Meshach, and Abednego were also promoted over Babylon and Media.[237] Is it not amazing how God set Jewish people over foreign kingdoms?! Truly, He raises up kings and throws kings down!

The 5th verse sounds so cruel to Christian ears. We must remember – the Jews were at war with their enemies. This was a civil war within the Persian Empire. By Mordecai's decree, the Jews were legally allowed to defend themselves against people who hated them enough to destroy them. Everything was at stake. This verse reads: "Thus the Jews defeated all their enemies with the stroke of the sword,

---

[236] See Genesis 41:40-44.
[237] See Daniel 2:48-49, 3:30, and 6:1-3.

with slaughter and destruction, and did what they pleased with those who hated them."

Apparently, one of the weapons used by the Jews was "the sword." This was a deadly weapon indeed. The word, "destruction," is also an intense word. But, once again, we must keep in mind where that word came from. Recall the wording from the Book of Esther: "Haman sought to *destroy* all the Jews" (3:6), "if it pleases the king, let a decree be written that they be *destroyed*" (3:9), "and the letters were sent by couriers into all the king's provinces, to *destroy*, to kill, and to annihilate all the Jews" (3:13), "the sum of money that Haman had promised to pay into the king's treasuries to *destroy* the Jews" (4:7), "Mordecai also gave Hathach (to give to Esther) a copy of the written decree for their *destruction*" (4:8), and "Haman, the son of Hammedatha the Agagite, the enemy of all the Jews, had plotted against the Jews to annihilate them, and had cast Pur (that is, the lot), to consume them and *destroy* them" (9:24). When Esther spoke to the king, listen to her language: "For we have been sold, my people and I, to be *destroyed*, to be killed, and to be annihilated" (7:4) and "how can I endure to see the *destruction* of my countrymen (8:6)?" We don't need to exonerate the actions of these Jews, but the "destruction" was first unleashed by Haman.

Regarding the last phrase of verse 5, I agree with Breneman who writes, "The expression 'they did what they pleased' should not be understood as a reference to cruelty but to the reversal of Haman's plans. The king had given him authority 'to do with the people as you please.'"[238] The turning of the tables is seen again. Perhaps Baldwin is correct also – "Do as they pleased – The inference is that the Jews were given a free hand without official interference."[239]

---

[238] See Breneman, page 359.
[239] See Baldwin, page 104.

Perhaps the "officials, satraps, and governors" "helped the Jews" by staying out of their way.

There must have been a lot of enemies in Shushan. "The Jews killed and destroyed five hundred men" (v6). This total is later officially confirmed by the king to Queen Esther in verse 12: "The Jews have killed and destroyed five hundred men in Shushan the citadel." The next day, they "killed three hundred men at Shushan" (v15). A total of 800 men were killed in Shushan alone.

The "multitude of his (Haman's) children" (5:11) is now clearly identified as "ten sons" (9:10, 9:12, 9:13, 9:14). For sure, "the ten sons of Haman" (v10) were enemies of the Jews. We are simply told that "they killed" them all. Again, King Ahasuerus confirms that "the ten sons of Haman" were killed in Shushan in verse 12. The names of the ten sons are listed in verses 7-9. We know nothing about them other than their names are of Persian origin. In a few verses, Esther will want them all hung on the fourteenth day. Jobes and Baldwin give salient reasons for their deaths: "This is another practice in ancient warfare. When a leader was killed, so was his entire family so that no one would survive to mount a vengeful coup"[240] and "the killing of Haman's ten sons forestalled any attempt on their part to avenge the death of their father or to usurp the office he had held."[241]

Mordecai's decree expressly permitted the Jews "to plunder their possessions" (8:11). Nevertheless, "they did not lay a hand on the plunder" (9:10) of the ten sons, "they did not lay a hand on the plunder" (9:15) of the 300 men, and "they did not lay a hand on the plunder" (9:16) of the 75,000 enemies. Why is this? "There was to be no personal profit in holy war because the destroyers were acting not on their own behalf but as agents of God's wrath."[242] "The author

---

[240] See Jobes, page 198.
[241] See Baldwin, page 104.
[242] See Jobes, page 196.

seeks to reverse the curse of King Saul and ensure blessing on Mordecai and his contemporaries. The deliberate decision not to enrich themselves at the expense of their enemies would not go unnoticed in a culture where victors were expected to take the spoil."[243]

Before we go to verses 11-14, we must recall that Mordecai's decree was valid only for "one day." Since there were more than five hundred enemies in Shushan, Esther needed official permission from the king to extend the deadline to the next day, the fourteenth. The Jews killed three hundred more.

The official government report that arrived at the king's palace was that "five hundred men and the ten sons of Haman" have been killed (v11). The king reports this information to Queen Esther, and as before, he asks the same questions: "Now what is your petition? It shall be granted to you. Or what is your further request? It shall be done" (v12). She still has his favor!

Esther 9:13-14 – "Then Esther said, 'If it pleases the king, let it be granted to the Jews who are in Shushan to do again tomorrow according to today's decree, and let Haman's ten sons be hanged on the gallows.' So the king commanded this to be done; the decree was issued in Shushan, and they hanged Haman's ten sons."

What she asks for has greatly bothered many modern readers and commentators. Many have accused Esther of pure, unadulterated brutality. Are they justified with these charges?

I believe that Esther was acting in her official capacity as a queen over the Persian Empire. Queen Esther was not authorizing more murders; no, she was in the middle of a war. The Jews had to defend themselves or be annihilated.

---

[243] See Baldwin, page 105.

When Timothy McVeigh, the dark perpetrator of the Oklahoma City bombing that killed 168 people including many children, was sentenced to death, many foolish and ignorant citizens of our country went to his execution site and held up signs that said "Thou shalt not kill." No! Thou shalt not kill was a commandment for Timothy McVeigh, not the governing authorities! The apostle Paul wrote in Romans 13:1-5, "Let every soul be subject to the governing authorities. For there is no authority except from God, and the authorities that exist are appointed by God. Therefore whoever resists the authority resists the ordinance of God, and those who resist will bring judgment on themselves. For rulers are not a terror to good works, but to evil. Do you want to be unafraid of the authority? Do what is good, and you will have praise from the same. For he is God's minister to you for good. But if you do evil, be afraid; for he does not bear the sword in vain; for he is God's minister, an avenger to execute wrath on him who practices evil. Therefore you must be subject, not only because of wrath but also for conscience' sake."

Esther was God's minister and avenger to execute wrath on those who practice evil. Even though Haman's ten sons were already dead, I believe Esther wanted them hung to let everyone know that this is the fate that awaits anyone who attacks the Jews. I agree with Swindoll who writes, "It was a way of saying publicly, 'What these men and their father stood for will never be allowed again!' There's a needed message of fear eloquently communicated in capital punishment."[244] And I disagree with Jobes that "Esther displays a surprising attitude of brutality."[245] Although difficult, Esther did what was necessary to protect her people and bring to nothing Haman's evil decree. Verse 16 says that the Jews "gathered together and protected their lives."

---

[244] See Swindoll, page 163.
[245] See Jobes, page 201.

In summary, the Jews killed "seventy-five thousand" in the "king's provinces," "five hundred men" "in Shushan the citadel," and "the ten sons of Haman" on the "thirteenth day of the month of Adar." Then they "killed three hundred men in Shushan" "on the fourteenth day of the month of Adar." In no case did they "lay a hand on the plunder."

Before we move on to the "gladness and feasting" of the rest of Esther Chapter 9, let's seriously consider how many people the Jews actually killed.

As with many numbers, dates, and genealogies in the Bible, we Christians have the habit of just reading over this detailed information without thinking through what has happened. Killing 75,500 people in one day is a huge number!

By way of comparison, let's consider some numbers of those killed during the American Civil War (1861-1865). The ten bloodiest Civil War battles had the follow numbers killed (including totals from both sides, the Union and  Confederate armies): Fredericksburg (5 days) (1,692), Stone's River (3 days) (2,971), 2nd Bull Run (3 days) (3,041), Chancellorsville (7 days) (3,271), Shiloh (2 days) (3,482), Antietam (1 day) (3,675), Wilderness (3 days) (3,723), Chickamauga (3 days) (3,969), Spotsylvania Courthouse (14 days) (4,240), and Gettysburg (3 days) (7,058). Remember, they were using rifles and cannon, fairly modern weapons. The total number of dead from all ten battles is 37,122 over 44 days. If you multiple this number by two, then you get almost 75,000. The Jews killed 75,500 in one day![246] Not even the atomic

---

[246] Yes, these totals involve people killed all over the vast Persian Empire. We are not told how these numbers were dispersed, but it should be assumed that many of the Jews were in Palestine, and much of the killing may have taken place there.

bombs dropped on the Japanese cities of Hiroshima and Nagasaki could match what the Jews did: Hiroshima, 45,000-60,000 dead (1st day) and Nagasaki, 19,000-25,000 dead (1st day).[247]

The Feast of Purim

Esther 9:17-18 are once again summary statements. The Jews "of the villages who dwelt in the unwalled towns" fought for one day – the 13th – and "rested" on the 14th. The Jews is Shushan fought for two days – the 13th and the 14th – so they "rested" on the 15th. Thus, the two days of celebration for the Feast of Purim are the 14th and 15th of Adar (March) (9:21). We begin our transition now to talking about the Feast of Purim. How and why was it established?

When all the fighting was over, I noticed right away that the narrator talks about "rest." The Jews "had *rest* from their enemies" (v16), "they *rested*" (v17) on the fourteenth, "they *rested*" (9:18) on the fifteenth, and "the Jews had *rest* from their enemies" (v22). Of course, then all the celebrations began. In three consecutive verses – 17, 18, and 19 – we read "they made it a day of feasting and gladness," "they made it a day of feasting and gladness," and "gladness and feasting, as a holiday, and for sending presents to one another."

Esther 9:20-28 explains how the Feast of Purim is established by Mordecai through another "written decree." The Persian Empire was a kingdom governed by laws and decrees. In these verses, we're going to see words like "Mordecai wrote these things," "sent letters," "to establish," "the custom which they had begun," "as Mordecai had written them," "he commanded by letter," "because of all the

---

[247] The long-term death totals from radiation poisoning and lingering sicknesses were 90,000-145,000 (Hiroshima) and 39,000-80,000 (Nagasaki). The estimates vary widely even from reputable sources. No one knows the final count.

words of this letter," and "according to the written instructions." The Feast of Purim would be "celebrated yearly on the fourteenth and fifteenth days of the month of Adar" (v21). This feast was to be celebrated because of the great reversal. What Haman intended for evil, God turned around for good.[248] In a verse that declares again God's invisible hand of blessing on the Jews, it says that their fate "was turned from sorrow to joy for them, and from mourning to a holiday; that they should make them days of feasting and joy, of sending presents to one another and gifts to the poor" (v22). "You see, they knew they were going to die. They knew it was coming...*until Almighty God sovereignly*

intervened. And now they chose the very days when they would have been annihilated and exterminated, and they turned those days from sadness and mourning to rejoicing and celebration to acknowledge the change of events."[249] Haman planned their extermination; God turned it into a celebration; the enemies wanted a slaughter; God turned it into laughter; a decree of one day to destroy, God turned it into two days of joy! God is good. "The day of death had come and gone and God's people were still alive!"[250]

Over and over again, I see the Lord turning terrible, wicked, and evil situations around for good. God is our Redeemer. What looks like an impending disaster turns out to be a blessing in disguise. Truly, in these moments of despair and uncertainty, we must "walk by faith and not by sight." I have seen countless situations in our local church where it appears that disaster has struck only to be turned

---

[248] Joseph told his brothers, "But as for you, you meant evil against me; but God meant it for good, in order to bring it about as it is this day, to save many people alive." See Genesis 50:20.
[249] See Swindoll, page 180.
[250] See Jobes, page 221.

around for the good of our people. Living with Christ always fills us with hope. No situation – no matter how dark – needs to overwhelm us. God turns the tables!

Earlier this year, my wife and I were vacationing in Sedona, Arizona and admiring the incredible and colorful rock formations that are part of that region. We drove down a back road to get to one of the national parks near our cabin where we were staying. There were crews working on the road we were traveling on. I noticed right away that these crews had put up orange cones to warn the drivers that they were putting black tar in the cracks of the road. Of course, I made sure that I did not drive anywhere near the tar because I didn't want any tar on my car's body, especially near the wheels. A few miles down the road, we stopped to take some pictures of the rock formations. When we walked back to the car, my wife noticed that black tar was all over the side of the car on the passenger side. I was so upset! I thought I went out of my way to avoid the tar; how did I get so much on the car? I tried to remove the fresh tar with a stick and some paper, but all to no avail. It only caused the tar to smear all over the paint. I was very frustrated and mad at myself. Why did I drive the car over the tar? I was mad at the construction crews. I was irritated at all the tar on the tires. My wife had to calm me down.

My wife then said, "Check the other side because there's probably tar on the driver's side of the car too." I was expecting the worst when I walked to the other side. But, thank God, it was all clean. There was tar only on the passenger side. As I looked closely at the driver's side front tire, I noticed something very unusual. When I had parked the car on the side of the road to take pictures, I had turned the front tires just enough to see more of the tread on them. I couldn't believe my eyes! There was a large chunk of tire missing from the front driver's side tire. I could actually see the steel radial wires. My tire was not far from blowing up! And just think, my wife and I had just driven over 600 miles from our home to Sedona on this vacation, and the speed limit in Arizona on most highways was 75 miles per hour! I immediately started thanking the Lord for sparing our life! To make a long story short, when we took the car to the auto repair shop, the manager told us that it's a miracle that the tire had not disintegrated at the speeds we were driving. Because we bought those tires from that same company in California, they gave us credit for the bad tire and went ahead and replaced all four tires for a very minimal cost.

The Lord made sure I got tar on my car. It forced me to inspect the car and see the chunk of tire that was missing. Now I found myself praising God for the tar! Now I thanked Him for the crews working that day out on the roads! Now I praised Him that the same company where I bought the tires in my hometown had the same store in this remote part of Arizona! We drove home on new tires and were safe. God turned what was bad into good! He is good!

Verse 25 gives us the conclusion: "This wicked plot which Haman had devised against the Jews should return on his own head, and that he and his sons should be hanged on the gallows." "People are caught in the traps they set for others."[251] Truly, those who curse the Jews are cursed.

"So the Jews accepted the custom which they had begun, as Mordecai had written to them" (v23). Esther 3:7 reads, "They cast Pur (that is, the lot) before Haman to determine the day and the month." As we taught in Chapter 3, the diviners (sorcerers) "rolled the dice" to determine the ominous day to carry out this annihilation. Esther 9:24 says that "Haman…had cast Pur (that is, the lot)." It adds, "So they called these days Purim, after the name Pur" (v26). The Hebrew word, "puwr," is found only in the Book of Esther.[252] The word is made plural by adding

---

[251] See Laniak, page 264.
[252] According to Laniak (page 266), "The term 'pur' comes from the Old Babylonian word 'puru' meaning 'fate' or 'lot.'"

the "im" at the end or "purim," meaning "lots."[253] There is a line in a song sung by modern-day Jews during the Feast of Purim that says "All the world was struck with amazement when Haman's pur became our Purim."[254] For the Jews, it went from death to life and from annihilation to celebration.

Esther 9:26-28 teaches that "the Jews established and imposed it upon themselves and their descendants and all who would join them, that without fail they should celebrate these two days every year" and it had to "be remembered and kept throughout every generation, every family, every province, and every city, that these days of Purim should not fail to be observed among the Jews, and that the memory of them should not perish among their descendants." For over 2,000 years now, the Jews have been celebrating this feast. "The celebration of Purim is therefore different from the feasts prescribed by the Torah. Rather than being imposed on the people from above as God's commandments, Purim began as the spontaneous response of God's people to His omnipotent faithfulness to the promises of the covenant."[255] Today's Jews read through the Book of Esther during the Feast of Purim to remind themselves continually of God's delivering power. They must never forget. They must always remember.

Adolf Hitler had a standing order that any Jew who had the Book of Esther in his or her possession was to be shot on the spot. He hated the book that gave the Jews their hope of deliverance.[256] Baldwin notes, "The threat which had been intended to annihilate the Jewish race became an occasion for uniting it, and Purim, like the other communal

---

[253] There are many well-known Hebrew words that have this ending. For example, seraphim, cherubim, Ephraim, Elohim, Gerizim, Zeboiim, Mahanaim, Urim, and Thummim.

[254] See Megillat Esther by R. Gordis, pages 93-97, quoted by Jobes, page 219.

[255] See Jobes, page 214.

[256] See Jobes' comments, page 220.

feasts, undoubtedly played its part in Jewish survival through the centuries in scattered geographical areas of Europe, Asia, and Africa, because it kept Jews apart from other people by its distinctiveness."[257]

In Esther 9:29-32, Queen Esther merely "confirms" what Mordecai had written about the establishment of the Feast of Purim among the Jews. In fact, we see this word repeatedly in these last verses – "With full authority to *confirm* this second letter about Purim" (v29), "to *confirm* these days of Purim" (v31), and "so the decree of Esther *confirmed* these matters of Purim" (v32).

In verse 29, we are reminded again that "Abihail"[258] was Esther's biological father, who was "the uncle of Mordecai" (2:15). It appears that "Queen Esther" "with Mordecai the Jew" wrote a joint statement regarding Purim, but as Jobes points out, "The Hebrew is clear in using the third person singular, feminine form of the verb, 'to write,' making it certain that Esther is the one who writes this final confirmation of Purim."[259] Jobes adds, "No other woman among God's people wrote with authority to confirm and establish a religious practice that still stands today. The importance of most biblical women, such as Sarah and Hannah, lies in their motherhood. Esther's importance to the covenant people in not as a mother, but as a queen."[260]

Most commentators are not sure what "this second letter" represents because Mordecai only wrote one letter or "this letter" according to verses 25-26.[261] In Esther 9:20 and 9:30, we find "Mordecai" sending "letters" to "all the Jews" "near and far, who were in all the provinces of King

---

[257] See Baldwin, page 109.

[258] "Abihail" in Hebrew means "father (possessor) of might."

[259] See Jobes, page 223.

[260] Ibid, page 224.

[261] The plural, "letters," of verses 20 and 30 appear to be just multiple copies of the same letter because they had to be sent to all 127 provinces or to Jews everywhere.

Ahasuerus" and "to the one hundred and twenty-seven provinces of the kingdom of Ahasuerus."

Thus, Mordecai wrote the decree establishing Purim and Esther confirmed it with yet another decree, so verse 31 declares that "Mordecai the Jew and Queen Esther" together "confirmed these days of Purim at their appointed time."

Verse 32 closes the longest chapter in Esther speaking about "the decree of Esther." "The form of the noun translated 'decree' is the same word previously used only in 1:15 to refer to the king's command to Vashti and in 2:20 to Mordecai's command to Esther. Apparently, the author's use of this word invites the reader to consider Queen Esther's word to be on par with that of Xerxes and Mordecai."[262] This decree was "written in the book." We're not told anything about "the book," so we don't know where exactly it was written. Perhaps it was "written in the book of the chronicles of Media and Persia" (10:2). See also the wording of Esther 2:23 and 6:1 – "...it was written in the book of the chronicles" and "...to bring the book of the records of the chronicles."

In conclusion, Haman built a gallows to hang Mordecai. He was hanged on it. Haman issued a decree to destroy all the Jews, and the Jews end up killing 75,800 of their enemies. This smashing victory results in the establishment of a celebration called the Feast of Purim whereby the Jews have been rejoicing over God's great deliverance from the hands of their enemies for over 2,000 years. Truly, the Lord "turned the sorrow to joy for them, and from mourning to a holiday; that they should make them days of feasting and joy" (9:22). This is the God we serve.

---

[262] See Jobes, page 223.

THE BOOK OF ESTHER

10

The Exaltation of Mordecai

*"For Mordecai the Jew was second to King
Ahasuerus, and was great among the Jews and
well received by the multitude of his brethren,
seeking the good of his people and speaking
peace to all his countrymen." (Esther 10:3)*

"The final chapter of Esther, which says
nothing about Esther, is a tribute to the
leadership of Mordecai."[263]   Baldwin
writes, "Miraculously, the power behind the throne of this
mighty empire was a Jew and therefore, though this is not
spelt out, one who feared God and stood for justice and right
in the affairs of state. Who would have expected that the
exiled Jews would ever have a representative in so
influential a position?"[264]

From the longest chapter to the shortest chapter, let's
take a look at Esther Chapter 10.

---

[263] See Laniak, page 267.
[264] See Baldwin, page 115.

Out of nowhere, this chapter begins with "And King Ahasuerus imposed tribute on the land and on the islands of the sea." Breneman comments, "Although he did not receive the great gift Haman had promised, King Xerxes prospered by receiving all this tribute."[265] The king got what he needed from taxes. He obtained this necessary tribute from the kingdom's "distant shores" or "the distant coastlands."[266] Just a few verses earlier, the king's government was described as "the kingdom of Ahasuerus" (9:30). It really was a "glorious kingdom" (1:4) that required a lot of money and resources to maintain. While Esther and Mordecai were issuing a decree to establish the Feast of Purim, the king was imposing tribute to establish the kingdom of Ahasuerus.

Verse 2 starts with "now all the acts of his power and his might" to describe King Ahasuerus. The acts have been "written in the book of the chronicles of the kings of Media and Persia." The Hebrew word here for "power" is the same one translated "authority" in 9:29 to speak about Esther writing with "full authority" to establish Purim. It is also used in Daniel 11:17 to explain "the strength" of a "kingdom." Despite his earlier disastrous military losses[267] to the Greeks, Ahasuerus's kingdom is strong and powerful. While he had to constantly put down rebellions throughout the vast empire, he was able to remain strong because of the tribute he collected regularly.

One of the reasons his kingdom was so strong was that Mordecai helped to govern the Persian Empire. "The king had advanced him." The Hebrew word here for "advanced" is the same one used when the king "promoted" Haman (3:1, 5:11). That the word is used nowhere else in the Book of Esther is again a reminder that Mordecai took Haman's position. Verse 2 also speaks of "the greatness of

---

[265] See Breneman, page 369.
[266] See the NIV and NLT translations.
[267] For example, at the Battle of Salamis in 480 B.C.

Mordecai." The beginning of his advance was when he saved the king's life. The king asked in 6:3, "What honor or *dignity* has been bestowed on Mordecai for this?" "Dignity" is the same Hebrew word found in 10:2 for "greatness" and is translated in other Old Testament verses as "great things."[268] Swindoll says, "The one who is exalted to the place of authority in Persia is a surprising choice. Who would have ever guessed that a Jew would become the prime minister in a Gentile land?"[269]

Esther 10:3 closes the book by telling us five things about "Mordecai the Jew." First, he was "second to King Ahasuerus." That a Jew could be promoted to the number two position in the powerful Persian Empire truly reveals Mordecai's "greatness." As both biblical and world history attest, the second in command is often the main mover and shaker in the government. Sometimes, kings act only as figure heads and the number two man runs the kingdom. This was true of Joseph before Pharaoh. Genesis 41:43 tells us that he rode in the "*second* chariot."[270]

I should say at this point that the number two man has to be someone of great trust and humility. There have been many "number two's" in biblical and world history who usurped the throne because the power went to their heads. Many Number 2's have wanted to be Number 1's. Through deception, intrigue, and violence, many kings and queens have been killed by their right-hand men. I have little doubt that if Haman had lived longer, he would have made a grab for the throne. He was a vain man filled with pride and arrogance. He would stop at nothing to sit on the throne alone!

Esther 8:15 says that "Mordecai" had a "great crown of gold" on his head; Esther 9:4 says, "Mordecai was great

---

[268] See, for example, 2 Samuel 7:21 and 7:23; 1 Chronicles 17:19.
[269] See Swindoll, page 188.
[270] The Hebrew word here for "second" is the same one used in Esther 10:3.

in the king's palace" and "this man Mordecai waxed greater and greater" (KJV). He was also "great among the Jews" (10:3). There is only one "Mordecai" in the Bible and he appears only in the Book of Esther, but since this book was written, thousands of Jews have named their male children, "Mordecai," because of his continuing fame and honor. For nearly 2,500 years, Mordecai has been "great among the Jews." "The greatness of Mordecai" is always seen first by his "greatness among the Jews."

Third, he was "well received by the multitude of his brethren" or he was "held in high esteem." This is the only place that "brothers" is used in the Book of Esther. This obviously means "his fellow Jewish brothers and sisters." The Hebrew word for "well received" is also translated as "delighted," "pleased," or "take pleasure in." Surely, Mordecai was a man of amazing integrity because who these days has that kind of reputation who works for the government?

It makes sense to me that the reason Mordecai was "well received" is because he was a person who was not focused on himself. He genuinely loved others and showed concern for their welfare. He was well received because he was always "seeking the good of his people." He wanted what was best for them. In today's world of political scandals and lies, it's difficult to find someone who is not grabbing for power, fame, and riches. People – both men and women – are in politics for themselves. Like the men at the Tower of Babel, they want to "make a name for themselves."[271] When I read about today's corrupt and inefficient politicians, it is amazing to read of Daniel that "the governors and satraps sought to find some charge against Daniel concerning the kingdom; but they could find no charge or fault, because he was faithful; nor was there any

---

[271] See Genesis 11:1-9, especially verse 4.

error or fault found in him."[272] Mordecai was a man like Daniel. He was faithful and he could not be corrupted. He was a man of integrity.

Finally, the book closes with these words: Mordecai was "speaking *peace* to all his countrymen." Esther 9:30 said that "Mordecai sent letters to all the Jews…with words of *peace* and truth." In both cases, the Hebrew words used is the famous, "shalom." Shalom is a very full word that is difficult to describe in English unless you use many different words. It is defined as "health, prosperity, safety, state of happiness, and well-being." It is a condition where someone is doing well in life and filled with joy. Mordecai was "speaking shalom" to his "countrymen." Interestingly, "countrymen" is translated nearly 230 times in the KJV translation as "seed," mostly referring to people's "descendants." In fact, it is translated "descendants" in Esther 9:27, 9:28, and 9:31. Zeresh said in Esther 6:13 (KJV), "If Mordecai be of the *seed* of the Jews…" Mordecai spoke well to his Jewish people, the "descendants" of Abraham, Isaac, and Jacob.

A Word About Greatness

Most Christians are afraid of the word, "great." The famous boxer, Muhammad Ali (1942-2016), told everyone, "I am the greatest." If I told you that "I am great" or "I am the greatest," you would immediately reject me as vain and conceited. Because we are all sinners and have fallen short of the glory of God, none of us can claim greatness for ourselves. Genesis 6:5 says correctly that "the Lord saw that the wickedness of man was great in the earth." About the only thing that's great is our wickedness. No one is great.[273]

---

[272] See Daniel 6:4.

[273] The only two men in the Old Testament that God said would be great or have a "great name" were Abraham and David (Genesis 12:2; 2 Samuel 5:10; 7:9; 1 Chronicles 17:8). Perhaps it is because these two

Only the Lord Jesus Christ is truly great.[274] The Psalms declare emphatically, "Great is the Lord, and greatly to be praised," "great is the Lord, and greatly to be praised; His greatness is unsearchable," and "bless the Lord, O my soul! O Lord my God, You are very great: You are clothed with honor and majesty."[275] Psalm 135:5 says, "For I know that the Lord is great." The Bible's praise book proclaims that God's "deliverance," "glory," "goodness," "mercy," "name," "wonders", and "works" are great. Everything about Him is great.

So how should Christians today talk about "the greatness of Mordecai" or that he was "great among the Jews?" Isn't that praising him too much? Isn't that putting him on a pedestal from which he could fall? Won't such adulation go to his head and eventually cause him to boast and fall like Haman? Is it not wisdom to take heed to Jeremiah's warning to the scribe, Baruch, when he asked, "Do you seek great things for yourself?" He answers his rhetorical question tersely, "Do not seek them."[276] Does not David's words in Psalm 131:1-2 resonate with the heart of the true servant of God: "My heart is not proud, O Lord, my eyes are not haughty; I do not concern myself with great matters or things too wonderful for me. But I have stilled and quieted my soul; like a weaned child with its mother, like a weaned child is my soul within me." Let us not seek after nor concern ourselves with great things.

---

men are uniquely associated with Jesus Christ as the "seed" and "son" of Abraham and David. In both cases, it was something God was going to do – "I will make your name great." In the New Testament, John the Baptist "would be great in the sight of the Lord" (Luke 1:15).

[274] See Luke 1:32. Jesus is our "great God and Savior" (Titus 2:13), "the great High Priest" (Hebrews 4:14), and "the great Shepherd of the sheep" (Hebrews 13:20).

[275] See Psalm 48:1, 145:3, and 104:1.

[276] See Jeremiah 45:5.

It was Martin Luther King Jr. (1929-1968), the famous civil rights leader, who said that "anyone can be great because anyone can serve." He was paraphrasing a truth taught by Jesus. The Lord said, "The greatest among you will be your servant. For whoever exalts himself will be humbled, and whoever humbles himself will be exalted."[277] Jesus also said, "Whoever desires to become great among you, let him be your servant, and whoever desires to be first among you, let him be your slave."[278] At one point, Jesus "took a little child and set him by Him," and then said, "For he who is least among you all will be great."[279] The Greek word here for "least" means "smallest." John the Baptist said in John 3:30, "He must increase, but I must decrease." Greatness in the kingdom of God involves getting smaller, becoming less, and decreasing. So much of what we see in today's churches involves Christians jockeying for position, proclaiming their greatness, and seeking bigger and better things. We're setting ourselves up for a fall.

Isn't it terribly sad that on two separate occasions, the Lord's own disciples broke out into arguing and fighting because they wanted to determine "which of them would be the greatest?"[280] What heightens the disappointment was that they had already asked Jesus, "Who then is greatest in the kingdom of heaven?" Jesus immediately called "a little child to Him, and set him in the midst of them." The Lord warned them, "Unless you are converted and become as little children" they would not enter the kingdom of heaven, for "whoever humbles himself as this little child is the greatest in the kingdom of heaven."[281] Greatness in the kingdom of the Lord means becoming like little children and servants of all. Greatness is definitely possible, but the way up is down,

---

[277] See Matthew 23:11-12.
[278] See also Matthew 20:26-27 and Mark 10:43-44.
[279] See Luke 9:47-48.
[280] See Luke 9:46 and 22:24.
[281] See Matthew 18:1-4.

becoming less is more, and humility brings exaltation. The one who teaches and does God's commandments and walks the way of humility – the Jesus way – "shall be called great in the kingdom of heaven."[282]

So let's go back to Mordecai. He was promoted. He was exalted. He was "advanced" by the king. "The king took off his signet ring and gave it to Mordecai" and "Esther appointed Mordecai over the house of Haman" (8:2); "Mordecai went out from the presence of the king in royal apparel of blue and white, with a great crown of gold and a garment of fine linen and purple" (8:15); "for Mordecai was great in the king's palace, and his fame spread throughout all the provinces; for this man Mordecai became more and more powerful" (9:4); and "for Mordecai the Jew was second to King Ahasuerus, and was great among the Jews" (10:3). Why should Christians be okay with his exaltation and greatness?

Well, first of all, when Mordecai saved the king's life and his honorable deed was written "in the presence of the king" (2:23), he made no effort to get a reward or be recognized. Then, after being recognized by the king through Haman as he was paraded through the streets of Shushan, when it was over, "Mordecai went back to the king's gate" (6:12). He asked for nothing more. He was not grabbing for any position or special reward. In fact, Mordecai says absolutely nothing in those critical 5th, 6th, and 7th chapters of Esther. Even after Haman is dead, Mordecai only came before the king because Esther "had told how he was related to her" (8:1). Mordecai was not seeking "great things for himself." He was not "concerned about great matters." He only concerned himself with "Esther's welfare and what was happening to her" (2:11). He remained "at the king's gate" probably acting in the capacity of a local judge. He was simply living out his life

---

[282] See Matthew 5:19.

as a God-fearing Jew in exile. He honored the Lord by his faithfulness, integrity, and devotion.

Mordecai is a model for today's church leader and Christian believer. Stay humble. Don't seek a title or position. Don't grab for the "chief seats" in the church. Stay low. Don't start counting numbers and telling everyone how great you are. These things diminish us as followers of Christ. Our reputation needs to be laid aside. The true call of greatness in the kingdom is "whatever you do, do all to the glory of God."[283] The prophet Malachi warned, "And now, O priests, this commandment is for you. If you will not hear, and if you will not take it to heart, *to give glory to My name*, says the Lord of hosts, I will send a curse upon you, and I will curse your blessings. Yes, I have cursed them already, because you do not take it to heart."[284] Let us take it to heart to give glory to His great name! Let us be like Mordecai who sought only to be a servant to the king, the queen, his fellow Jews, and the citizens of the Persian Empire.

---

[283] See 1 Corinthians 10:31.
[284] See Malachi 2:1-2.

THE BOOK OF ESTHER

Esther Chapter 1 – Study Questions

Read 2 Chronicles 36:22-23; Ezra 1:1-2; and Isaiah 44:28-45:1. The Lord raised up Cyrus the Persian king. Summarize *briefly* what these verses say that King Cyrus did:

Read Daniel 2:32 and 2:39, Daniel 7:5, and Daniel 8:3-4 and 8:20. Summarize *briefly* what these dreams and visions predicted about the coming Medo-Persian Empire?:

As you read Esther 1:1-4, highlight at least three features of King Ahasuerus' kingdom and realm:

As you read Esther 1:16-18, what was the basis of Memucan's argument against Queen Vashti?:

Esther Chapter 2 – Study Questions

Who was Mordecai and how did he and his forefathers end up in Babylon and ultimately Persia? See Esther 2:5-6; 2 Kings 24:13-16:

What do we know about Esther from verses like Esther 2:7, 2:15, and 9:29?:

Besides her incredible beauty, there was something else even more important for why Esther was chosen queen over all the other beautiful ladies of the Persian kingdom. What was it and how does this reveal God's invisible hand behind the scenes? See Esther 2:8-18:

How do Mordecai's "chance" encounter with two would-be assassins and Mordecai's "delayed honor" reveal the hand of God working behind the scenes. See Esther 2:21-23, 6:1-3:

Using the teaching in the introduction on the foreknowledge and providence of God, describe what that means for your own life. If necessary, give a personal example from your own life of God's supernatural "providence":

Esther Chapter 3 – Study Questions

As you read Exodus 17:13-16 and Deuteronomy 25:17-19, what is the Lord's attitude and purpose toward the Amalekites?:

Mordecai was a "son of Kish, a Benjaminite" (2:5-6) and Haman was an "Agagite" (3:1) or Amalekite. In reading, 1 Samuel Chapter 15, what can we say about the clash of these two life-long enemies as they meet here in the Book of Esther:

Mordecai could have spared himself a lot of trouble if he had just bowed to Haman. Why wouldn't he bow or give homage to Haman in Esther 3:2-5?:

Summarize briefly how Haman was able to propose and decree the extermination of all Jews in Esther 3:6-10?:

Esther Chapter 4 – Study Questions

What was the reaction of Mordecai and the Jews to Haman's decree in Esther 4:1-3?:

How did Esther become aware of Haman's plot according to Esther 4:4-9?:

Why was Esther initially hesitant to go talk to the king and how did Mordecai convince her to go according to Esther 4:4-12?:

How can a believer today see the providence of God in Esther, Chapters 3-4?:

If God is working everything out according to His will, why should Christians today continue to pray and fast? If God is overseeing everything, and reigning sovereignly to accomplish His purposes, how will prayer make any difference?:

Esther Chapter 5 – Study Questions

As you read Esther 5:1-6, how do you know that Esther was walking in faith and with God's favor?:

In your view, why didn't Esther tell the king her nationality and about Haman's evil plan if she already had his favor? (Esther 5:6-8):

How does Esther 5:11-12 reveal Haman's pride and arrogance?:

What is the main lesson you learned in this chapter of the Book of Esther? How can you apply it into your Christian life?:

Esther Chapter 6 – Study Questions

As you read Esther 6:1-6, what happens here that reveals God's providence and His workings behind the scenes?:

The Bible says repeatedly that "pride goes before destruction and a haughty spirit before a fall" and "whoever exalts himself will be humbled, and whoever humbles himself will be exalted." Summarize how these truths are seen in Esther 6:6-14:

As you look over Esther, Chapters 5-6, how do the events in these two chapters assure you that now everything is ready for Esther's second banquet in Chapter 7, where she tells the king her petition and request?:

How has Mordecai's "Jewish descent" (6:13) played a key role in the story found here in Esther Chapters 5-6? See 5:13 and 6:10 also:

Why is the word "prepared" such a key word in Chapters 5-7 of Esther? See 5:4, 5:5, 5:8, 5:12, 6:4, 6:14, and 7:10:

Esther Chapter 7 – Study Questions

The word, "favor," is mentioned seven times in the Book of Esther, and each one is associated with Queen Esther. She had the favor of God. See Esther 2:9, 2:15, 2:17, 5:2, 5:8, 7:3, and 8:5. Exactly how does a Christian obtain God's favor?:

Read Psalm 7:15-16, Proverbs 26:27, and Ecclesiastes 10:8. These verses teach that "whoever digs a pit falls into it." How was this fulfilled in Haman's life? (Esther 7:10):

At just the right time, God used the king's eunuchs (unbelievers) to accomplish His purposes in the Book of Esther – "Harbonah" (Esther 7:9); "Hathach" (4:5-10); "Hegai" (2:15); and "Shaashgaz" (2:14). What does this tell us about God's power and sovereignty over the affairs of men?:

What is the main lesson you learned in this seventh chapter of Esther? How can you apply it to your own life?:

Esther Chapter 8 – Study Questions

What happened to the "house/estate of Haman" after he was hanged? See Esther 8:1-2, 7:

In Esther 8:3-6, how did Esther avoid blaming the king for the decree that was signed with his own signet ring and place the blame squarely on "Haman the Agagite":

Summarize briefly how the edict issued by Mordecai was sent to all the provinces in the Persian Empire. See Esther 8:8-10, 8:14:

As we compare Haman's decree (3:12-13) with Mordecai's decree (8:11-13), why should we not see Mordecai's as an act of revenge that is forbidden in Scripture (see Romans 12:17-21, for example):

Esther Chapters 9 & 10 – Study Questions

Why were the Jews able to defeat their enemies according to Esther 9:2-5?:

Why was it important to kill Haman's sons and what purpose did Esther have in hanging them after they were already dead? (Esther 9:6-14):

In the following verses we see these important words: "The Jews gathered together" (8:11), "the Jews gathered together" (9:2), "the Jews gathered together again" (9:15), "the remainder of the Jews gathered together" (9:16), and "the Jews assembled together" (9:18). What can Christians learn from this example when we are being attacked by our enemies?:

Summarize how the feast of Purim was established on the "fourteenth and fifteenth days" of the month of Adar according to Esther 9:17-22:

Mordecai was a God-fearing Jew who never sought position, power, or greatness, and yet, God exalted him to the highest position in the Persian Empire after the king (see Esther 8:2, 8:15, 9:4, and 10:2-3). What lessons can Christians today learn about humility and pride from Mordecai's example?:

About the Author

Charlie Avila is the Senior Pastor of Clovis Christian Center in Fresno, California. He is married to Irma and has two adult children – Leah and Daniel. Pastor Charlie is the Bible teacher of the Spirit of Wisdom and Revelation teaching newsletters and the principal teacher on the Teacher of the Bible website.

He is an instructor with the Fresno School of Mission and other ministry schools. He teaches special seminars on various Bible subjects and verse by verse studies through Old Testament and New Testament books. He has written several books available on Amazon including *The Christian and Anger, The Christian and Homosexuality, The Christian and Hell, Detecting & Dealing with False Teachings* and various commentaries on books of the Bible. He also has books in Spanish by the same titles as the English versions.

He can be contacted at teacherofthebible@gmail.com or Clovis Christian Center, 3606 N. Fowler Ave, Fresno, CA 93727-1124.

The MP3 audio, video, lecture notes and homework (PDF), and PowerPoint for the complete lecture series on the Book of Esther is available at www.teacherofthebible.com. The videos are also available on YouTube. Just type "Esther Pastor Charlie Avila" on the search line.

THE BOOK OF ESTHER

Selected Bibliography
(By Author)

Esther: An Introduction & Commentary, **Joyce G. Baldwin, Tyndale Old Testament Commentaries, Inter-Varsity Press, Downers Grove, Illinois.**

Joyce G. Baldwin (1921-1995) was a British evangelical teacher and former dean of women at Trinity College in Bristol, England. I have read through other Old Testament commentaries that she has written, including the ones on the books of Daniel, Haggai, and Malachi. She has always presented sound, conservative teachings in her studies.

Back in the late 1960s she began to do detailed studies on books that had women as the primary character. Thus, she studied Ruth and Esther.

Her commentary on Esther is 126 pages long. Her Introduction was quite long – forty pages – and provided good background information on the book. This is followed by a short, 2-page outline of Esther that was very generic in nature. Pages 55-116 provide a verse by verse study of all ten chapters of Esther. At the end, she includes a 7-page Appendix entitled, "The Greek Additions," which contains the additional sections of Esther that were added as part of the Greek Septuagint and included in *The Jerusalem Bible.*

I read all the way through Baldwin's commentary before I read any other book and before I taught the class. It gave me a good basic framework of the book and its historical background.

The best part of her commentary was her comments on Esther Chapter 9. I quoted from this section a lot during my lecture on that chapter. Like Dr. Karen Jobes, I was interested to hear a Christian woman/interpreter speak on the female issues of Esther. For example, like how King Ahasuerus treated women, both Vashti and Esther, and all the ladies who tried out for the "Miss Persia Beauty Contest" in Esther 2. Again, her comments were fair and interpreted in light of the Persian culture of that time.

At the end of several chapters, she includes "Additional Notes" on Hebrew words or specific topics that may be of interest to the general reader. These include notes on "Fasting" at the end of Chapter 4; the Hebrew word, "naqam," or "avenge; vengeance," after Chapter 8; and the word, "menot," or "portions" after Chapter 9. These comments were not entirely useful to the overall understanding of the book. I did like her title for Esther Chapter 6 – *"Haman Inadvertently Promotes Mordecai"* (page 88).

Though it was not the best commentary on Esther, it was still good. I would give it a "B" or 8 out of 10.

***Ezra, Nehemiah, Esther,* Mervin Breneman, The New American Commentary, An Exegetical and Theological Exposition of Holy Scripture, Broadman and Holman Publishers, Nashville, Tennessee.**

 Mervin Breneman is a Professor of Old Testament at the Seminario Internacional Teológico Bautista in Buenos Aires, Argentina. He received a B.A. in New Testament Greek and M.A. in Theology from Wheaton College. He also holds a M.A. and Ph.D. from Brandeis University. He has written, along with others, a commentary in Spanish on Psalms, and another book based on the Ten Commandments entitled *The Will of God for your Daily Life*, also written in Spanish.

The New American Commentary that I used also includes commentaries on Ezra and Nehemiah. I have not read those sections so I cannot comment on them. The Esther portion of this commentary covers pages 277-370. His Introduction was twenty-two pages long, and like Baldwin, was followed by a brief 2-page outline. The

Introduction was not remarkable, but did include some modern considerations like *The Dangers of Anti-Semitism* and *The Providence of God.* The book includes three indexes including Subject Index, Person Index, and a Selected Scripture Index which were very thorough. It was surprising to see that Breneman included no bibliography for all three Bible books – Ezra, Nehemiah, and Esther.

In his commentary, I found his teaching on the "preparation" of Esther's banquet on Esther Chapter 5, his comments on Chapter 8, and his overall teaching on Anti-Semitism to be very good. I found Breneman's commentary much like Baldwin's. He always provided sound teaching, but many of the chapters lacked any punch. I was left wanting more.

Overall, I would give this commentary a B-. Maybe an 8 out of 10. If you only had to buy one commentary, I would look elsewhere (I recommend Jobes).

1-2 Kings, 1-2 Chronicles, Ezra, Nehemiah, Esther, Ancient Christian Commentary on Scripture, Old Testament Volume V, Edited by Marco Conti, InterVarsity Press, Downers Grove, Illinois.

This book is Volume V of the Ancient Commentary of Scripture (ACS) Series. It includes comments on six other Old Testament books. The Esther section of this book covers pages 374-399.

The editor for this volume is Dr. Marco Conti. He received his Ph.D. from the University of Leeds, which is located north of London near Manchester. Conti is a professor of medieval and humanistic Latin literature at the Ateneo Salesiano and lecturer in classical mythology and religions of the Roman Empire at Richmond University in Rome. He is the coeditor of the volume on Job in this series and provided translation assistance for other volumes as well.

Although there are comments from early church fathers like Jerome, Clement of Alexandria, Ambrose, and Origen, most of the "ancient commentary" is from Rabanus Maurus (780-856). Maurus was a Frankish monk, theologian, and teacher who is technically an early medieval writer. He wrote commentaries on Bible books like 1 and 2 Kings and Esther. He was also the author of poetry, homilies, an encyclopedia, and treatises on education and doctrine.

I'll get right to the point: Maurus' comments, like many people after Origen, are filled with allegorical interpretations of the biblical text. He likes to use the words, "spiritual meaning" or "it signifies." This is always a disastrous way to interpret the Bible (see also my comments on Stedman's book). For example, Maurus says that the two eunuchs who tried to assassinate King Ahasuerus "signified" the "Scribes and Pharisees of the Jews" (page 380). Esther "signifies the gentile church" and Mordecai "the future teachers of the Gentiles" (page 379). Whenever Haman does anything in Esther, Maurus gives it an "allegorical interpretation" (page 382). When Esther falls at the feet of King Ahasuerus in Esther Chapter 8, Maurus says that this "plainly symbolizes" the holy church bowing at the feet of Jesus (page 393). The "mounted couriers" who take the decrees throughout the Persian Empire in Chapter 8 are "the holy preachers" who will take the gospel throughout the world. So, Maurus cannot take the plain historical reading of the text and teach us something useful. No, he has to "spiritualize" it and get it to "represent" something else.

I found almost nothing useful or quotable in the twenty-five pages of commentary. This ancient commentary on Esther should have stayed ancient and hidden away in some medieval monastery. I like to write comments in the books that I'm reading for future reference, and I found myself writing the word, "False," on several margins of this commentary. I don't like to say that, but it's the truth.

I do not recommend the Esther portion of this commentary. I haven't read too much of the other books in this commentary, so I can't give any feedback on them, but I definitely would not use comments by Rabanus Maurus unless someone wanted to teach others on how *not* to interpret Scripture.

I give this book an F. Please look somewhere else if you want to learn something from the Book of Esther.

Esther, Karen H. Jobes, The NIV Application Commentary, Zondervan Publishers, Grand Rapids, Michigan.

You can learn more about the author at her own website, karenjobes.com. She originally started out with degrees in physics and computer science and worked in those fields at Princeton University and Johnson & Johnson. Her husband was a plasma physicist at Princeton. She later got a Ph.D. at the Westminster Theological Seminary and fell in love with the Reformed Faith. She has been an assistant professor of New Testament Studies at Westmont College in Santa Barbara, California and recently finished eleven years (2005-2015) as the Gerald F. Hawthorne Professor of New Testament Greek and Exegesis at Wheaton College and Graduate School in Wheaton, Illinois.

She has written outstanding commentaries on 1 Peter through Baker Publishing and another one on the epistles of John (1, 2, and 3) through Zondervan. Both commentaries have received rave reviews from various ministers and publishing companies.

After doing some on-line research on the best commentaries on Esther, nearly everyone had Jobes' commentary at the top. After reading all of her commentary, I have to agree with others – this is the best commentary on Esther that I have read.

Her commentary is 242 pages long and the Introduction is thirty pages long. It includes a Scripture and General Index in the back. I really liked this book because it was not just of academic interest, but included a lot of sections on "contemporary significance." She writes very well and uses a lot of examples as illustrations. She also had a 2-page outline with a good "annotated bibliography" that included commentaries, historical issues, Persian Period History, and books on "the Doctrine of Divine Providence," which is the heart of Esther. There is a very good "Theological Postscript" at the end on "The Doctrine of Divine Providence," which summarized well the main theme of Esther.

As with all commentaries in the *NIV Application Commentary* series, each section was broken down into three areas – Original Meaning, Building Contexts, and Contemporary Significance. At every point and in every section, Jobes provided excellent commentary and historical background. I especially liked how she taught that Christians today cannot interpret some of King Ahasuerus' actions through New Testament truths about "husbands loving your wives as Christ loved the church." The king was not living as a Christian nor with the teachings of the apostle Paul. He lived as a powerful dictator over one of the greatest kingdoms in world history. He ruled by decree (as the Book of Esther makes abundantly clear). His actions with queens and concubines must be interpreted in that light. Jobes keeps this balance throughout her commentary.

Perhaps other than Laniak's commentary, I quoted more from this book than any others. Jobes is a very good writer and states her views clearly. Probably the best part of the book was her interpretation of Chapter 7.

Although I have not read all the commentaries on Esther, this is clearly an excellent commentary on Esther. I recommend all students of the Word of God to study this book. I give it an A or 9.5 out of 10.

Ezra, Nehemiah, Esther, Leslie Allen and Timothy Laniak, New International Biblical Commentary, Hendrickson Publishers, Peabody, Massachusetts.

Dr. Tim Laniak serves at the Gordon-Conwell Theological Seminary in Charlotte, North Carolina as the Dean, Professor of Old Testament, and Mentor for the Christian Leadership Doctor of Ministry Track. He received his bachelor's degree from Wheaton College, his M.Div. from Gordon-Conwell Seminary, and his doctorate in Old Testament and Early Judaism from Harvard Divinity School. Dr. Laniak has published a book on social anthropology and the Bible (*Shame and Honor in the Book of Esther*, Scholars Press, 1997).

This *New International Biblical Commentary* (NIBC) volume includes the books of Ezra, Nehemiah, and Esther. Dr. Leslie Allen wrote the sections on Ezra and Nehemiah, while Dr. Laniak did the commentary on Esther. The Esther portion covers pages 167-269, so it is just over 100 pages long.

His Introduction was nearly twenty-five pages long and provided a lot of good background information. While I was studying this book as part of the course preparation for my Esther class that I did at our School of Ministry, I found myself writing phrases like "excellent wording" and "lots of good word searches" along the margins. I was amazed at how often Laniak found various key words in Esther and brought out their significance to the overall structure of the book. This was perhaps the best part of the commentary.

As with all volumes in the NIBC series, this one includes a verse by verse commentary followed by an "Additional Notes" section that usually provides additional technical information on the Hebrew text or the meaning/significance of any phrases or words. Again, Dr. Laniak has a very sharp eye for Esther's use of certain keys words, and he brings out how these words are used throughout the Book of Esther.

Both Allen and Laniak provide a "For Further Reading" section that includes commentaries and special studies on Ezra, Nehemiah, and Esther. This is followed by a Subject and Scripture Index.

The best part of the commentary is the section on Esther Chapter 7. I love the sentence – "Her enemy is now his enemy and thus The Enemy" (page 244) – when Esther exposes Haman's plan to the king.

Overall, I would give this commentary an A- or 9 out of 10. It provides excellent comments throughout and much quotable material. Along with Jobes' commentary, it was the best among the commentaries that I studied.

***Five Smooth Stones for Pastoral Work*, Eugene H. Peterson, The Pastoral Work of Community-Building: Esther, Eerdmans Publishing Company, Grand Rapids, Michigan.**

Eugene Hoiland Peterson (1932-2018), the prolific writer and author/interpreter of the popular *The Message* paraphrase of the Bible, died just a few days after we finished our course on Esther. He was an American Presbyterian clergyman, scholar, theologian, author, and poet.

The hardcover book that I used was called Eugene Peterson's *Pastoral Library* – Four Books in One Volume. The first book is called *Five Smooth Stones for Pastoral Work*, which includes "pastoral insights" from Song of Songs, Ruth, Lamentations, Ecclesiastes, and Esther. The section on Esther covered pages 191 to 237. This study of Esther was called *The Pastoral Work of Community-Building*.

This is definitely not a verse by verse commentary of Esther, but it is an excellent study on "community building." It really opened my eyes to how the Jews worked together to defeat their enemies in those last chapters of Esther, especially Chapter 9. As I wrote in my commentary: It is easy to miss the first key element of the Jews' victory found in verse 2. Observe these simple, but powerful, words: "The Jews who were in every city *gathered together*" (8:11), "the Jews *gathered together* in their cities" (9:2), "the Jews who were in Shushan *gathered together* again" (9:15), "the Jews in the king's provinces *gathered together*" (9:16), and "the Jews who were at Shushan *assembled together*" (9:18). *When God's people are attacked, they must "gather together."* This is going to be the key to victory for the last-days' church.

I used this important truth recently to rally many believers around a Christian leader who was under attack. We prayed together and saw God's mighty deliverance on his behalf.

Peterson is a master of words. I like when he writes, "Wherever there is a people of God there are enemies of God." Also, he made some powerful statements about Mordecai's character that definitely helped me teach on his life: "His leadership was an outgrowth of what he was: he did not set himself up to lead; he did not aspire to leadership; he was, simply, 'a Jew.' By living consistently within that identity and doing the duties that went with it, he fulfilled the functions of leadership: raising his uncle's daughter, keeping the First Commandment, interceding for his people, and trusting in God. Leadership, for Mordecai, was not self-assertion, not ego-fulfillment, but being a man of God and doing whatever flowed naturally from that traditional identity" (page 226).

If you want a verse by verse commentary, you'll have to look elsewhere, but if you're interested in some good insights on the community of the Jews in Persia and pastoral leadership today, I recommend this volume. I give it a B+ or 8.8 out of 10.

For Such a Time as This: Secrets of Strategic Living from the Book of Esther, Ray C. Stedman, Discovery House Publishers, Grand Rapids, Michigan.

Raymond Charles Stedman (1917-1992) was an evangelical pastor and prolific author. He was the long-time pastor of Peninsula Bible Church in Palo Alto, California, and author of many books. This devotional study is 153 pages long.

First of all, let me say that Pastor Stedman was a minister who was greatly respected by many people and served the Lord faithfully for forty years as a pastor at his church in Palo Alto. Recently, Mark Mitchell wrote a book entitled *Portrait of Integrity – The Life of Ray C. Stedman.* He has written dozens of books providing spiritual insights into many books of the Bible. His messages have reached millions of people everywhere.

I have other books in my library from Pastor Stedman, including his bestselling classic, *Authentic Christianity*, and his devotional commentary on Ecclesiastes, *Is This All There is to Life?* I learned much from these books.

I bought his devotional commentary on Esther for this reason. I have received so much from him in the past, that I thought I would surely enjoy his study on Esther. Being a Bible teacher and researcher, I often get bored with Old Testament commentaries that are heavy on Hebrew words and obscure observations about some extra-biblical source. I need practical wisdom useful as a pastor who needs to teach the sheep. I was wholeheartedly expecting this from Stedman's book.

Wow, was I disappointed! This book became one of my worst nightmares. I'm actually going to use it at my next

False Teaching Seminar to train future pastors how not to interpret Scripture. In one word, this book was a *disaster*. I mean a real, full-blown disaster of biblical interpretation. It pains me to write this because I know so many people love and respect Pastor Stedman, but I cannot deny what I read in this devotional study.

What he writes about God, Jesus, and the Holy Spirit are true and accurate. That's not the problem. What he does throughout his book is spiritualize everything in Esther. Getting right to the point, he says that Haman represents "the flesh," Mordecai symbolizes the "Holy Spirit," the Jews in Esther are the "fruit of the Spirit," and the three days of fasting in Esther 4 represent the resurrection of Jesus Christ on the third day! Also, King Ahasuerus represents the "soul" with its "mind, emotions, and will." The summary statement of his beliefs can be found on page 67: "The story of Esther can be seen as a divinely inspired portrayal of the spiritual principles that govern your life and mine in these times in which we live." He doesn't use the Book of Esther as a historical narrative that actually took place about 2,500 years ago in the Persia Empire. He turns everything and everyone into "spiritual principles." As with Origen who spiritualized and allegorized the Bible text to death, you can get the Bible to say whatever you want it to say. This is a terrible form of exegesis.

Listen to what he writes when writing about King Ahasuerus: "By way of analogy, you are the king of your own kingdom. The empire of your life reaches out and has an impact on all who come in contact with you. If you are a Christian, then you found a new 'queen' (i.e. Esther) when your spirit was made alive in Jesus Christ. You became aware of the influence of the Holy Spirit (Mordecai), who has recorded in a book the story of an evil plot against your life. This is how the story of Esther retraces the story of your life" (page 42). Later on, in interpreting Esther Chapter 8, when "Mordecai is brought into the presence of the king," he says that this means it "symbolizes the moment that the soul becomes conscious of the presence of the Holy Spirit and becomes aware of the need to submit to the Spirit's wisdom and authority" (pages 106-107). This makes no sense because earlier, in page 46, he wrote, "The 'Mordecai' in our lives is the Holy Spirit." Mordecai as the Holy Spirit submits to King Ahasuerus as the Holy Spirit. Very confusing!

Now, what he writes in general about the flesh, Holy Spirit, Jesus, and the church is correct, but you can't make the Book of Esther say things spiritually that it was never intended to say. It's the way many early church fathers interpreted the Song of Songs that has destroyed the truth of that book for nearly two thousand years. And we wonder why so many Christians have problems with their marriages and sexuality! It's the knowledge of the truth that sets us free. Errors and lies bind us up. Satan is the great deceiver and liar.

About the only thing I liked from Stedman's book was the title to Esther Chapter 7, which he called, "Haman's Last Supper" (page 93).

I'm sorry Ray Stedman fans, I have to give this book an F, and I don't recommend that Christians read it. We don't interpret the Book of Esther by spiritualizing everything and saying that certain people in the story represent spiritual things.

Esther: A Woman of Strength & Dignity, **Charles R. Swindoll, Word Publishing, Nashville, Tennessee.**

Charles Rozell "Chuck" Swindoll is an evangelical Christian pastor, author, educator, and radio preacher. He founded *Insight for Living*, headquartered in Frisco, Texas, which airs a radio program of the same name on more than 2,000 stations around the world in 15

languages. He was born in Texas in 1934. His website is insight.org.

His devotional study on Esther is from his "Profiles in Character" or "Great Lives from God's Word" series. This book is 198 pages long.

As I mentioned previously, I didn't want to use only biblical commentaries from Hebrew scholars while preparing for my Esther class. I need pastoral wisdom so I can feed God's flock. Too many commentaries are big on the technical nuisances of the text but not very big on insights for practical living. I was hoping that this devotional study would do just that, and certainly after the big disappointment in Stedman's book.

I like how Swindoll defines divine providence at the beginning of the book. It gave me great insights on how to begin my class on the first day. "Providence is seeing ahead of time" (page 6). Certainly, this is the theme throughout Esther – God saw everything in advance and made necessary plans to save God's people. His first chapter entitled *God's Invisible Providence* was very good, and helped me to state the main theme of Esther at the beginning of my course.

I think the best part of the book was his comments on Esther Chapter 2 during the "Miss Persia" contest, as he calls it. Swindoll gives us the necessary background to see how "divine providence" worked out Esther's selection as queen over the Persian Empire. I also liked his insights at the end of Chapter 2 and beginning of Chapter 3, when Mordecai is overlooked for honor by the king but instead promotes Haman. This again reveals God's invisible hand in the affairs of men. Some of the later chapters of his book were a little mundane and I didn't get too much out of them.

Unlike Stedman, Chuck Swindoll does draw out some good principles for living from Esther. He did a good job of showing how humility was working in the lives of Mordecai and Esther. Overall, I would give this book a B or

8 out of 10. If you want something other than a true verse by verse commentary, then this book is good.

***Persia and the Bible*, Edwin M. Yamauchi, Baker Books, Grand Rapids, Michigan.**

Dr. Edwin Masao Yamauchi is a Japanese-American historian, Christian apologist, editor and academic. He is Professor Emeritus of History at Miami University, where he taught from 1969 until 2005. He was initially educated at the University of Hawaii, but then transferred and obtained his Bachelor's Degree at Shelton College. He later received his M.A. and Ph.D. from Brandeis University.

One of the top Christians experts on languages, he has worked with ancient near eastern languages, including Hebrew, Aramaic, Akkadian, Ugaritic, Arabic, Syriac, and Coptic. In all, he has immersed himself in 22 different languages.

His book, *Persia and the Bible*, is a classic in its field. Anyone who wants to do a comprehensive study on Persia from a biblical perspective needs this book. It is a wealth of learning and filled with incredible, but readable, details of the Persians and their empire. The book is nearly 600 pages long and has an extensive "Selected Bibliography" of twenty-two pages, small print, double-columns! There are also four indexes: Index of Subjects, Index of Places, Index of Authors, and Index of Scripture. Very comprehensive.

The chapters include Persian kings and Persian cities. For example, Chapter 2 through 6 include detailed studies on Cyrus, Cambyses, Darius, Xerxes, and Artaxerxes. The "city chapters" include Susa, Ecbatana, Pasargadae, and Persepolis. There are also chapters on "The Medes," "Persia and the Greeks," "The Magi," and "Zoroastrianism."

Because of my study of Esther, I spent most of my time studying the chapters on Darius and Xerxes. The chapter on Xerxes also included an excellent section on "The Persian Background of Esther." He gave good background information on Vashti, King Ahasuerus, Queen Esther, Haman, and Mordecai. His book is peppered throughout with maps, drawings, diagrams, paintings, pottery, and pictures of statues and temples. The back-cover states that there are over 100 such items in the book. I really liked the historical information that he gave on the Persian and Greek battles. This historical information provides the background to the early chapters of Esther.

While Yamauchi's book is not a verse by verse commentary, it is an excellent reference – encyclopedia if you will – into the Persian Empire and its culture. I'm glad I own this book as I will use it in the future in my studies of biblical books like Daniel and Nehemiah, both of which deal with the Persians.

For its background information on Persia, I give this book an A; for its teaching on Esther, I give it a B. I recommend this book highly as a reference source to the Persian Empire. There is no other book that is better – it is well written and easy to follow.

THE BOOK OF ESTHER

Scriptural Reference Index

Made in the USA
Monee, IL
20 January 2024